THE OREGON TRAIL

A PHOTOGRAPHIC JOURNEY

THE OREGON TRAIL

A PHOTOGRAPHIC JOURNEY

Bill and Jan Moeller

For Bonnie — we truly could not have done it without her,
and for Don, who is always unfailingly enthusiastic about our work.

PUBLISHER
BEAUTIFUL AMERICA PUBLISHING CO.
9725 S.W. Commerce Circle
Wilsonville, Oregon 97070

Library of Congress Catalog Card Number 85-28787

––––––––––––––––––

ISBN: 089802-442-0

DESIGN: Patrick H. Kolb
LAYOUT: Karen S. Keil
TYPESETTING: Oregon Typesetting
PRINTING: In Korea through Creative Graphics International, Inc., New York, N.Y.
FIRST EDITION: December, 1985

ACKNOWLEDGEMENTS

So many people helped us with this book in ways large and small, sometimes knowingly, sometimes not; to them all we owe our thanks.

When the project was germinating in our minds, the first one who encouraged us to go ahead was Nancy Wilson, curator of the McLoughlin House in Oregon City. She steered us in many helpful directions, one of which was to Joleen P. Jensen, at the Oregon Historical Society, who provided us with much needed data in the beginning.

Since the book is done chronologically along the Oregon Trail, here, listed in the same order, are those who provided us with assistance and information: Wayne Brandt and his staff at Rock Creek Station State Historical Park, and, especially, Todd Brauch, who drove the oxen in the best pioneer fashion; Estaline Carpenter and Lester Jones of the Jefferson County Historical Society; Eugene Hunt, Superintendent, Fort Kearny State Historical Park; Steve Scheinost for his information regarding California Hill; Dennis Shimmin, Superintendent, Ash Hollow State Historical Park; Jerry Banta, Superintendent, and the staff at Scott's Bluff National Monument who tirelessly answered all our many questions, and Mert Davis who was barraged with most of the thorny ones and never failed to come up with the answers; Gary K. Howe, Superintendent, Fort Laramie National Historic Site, who allowed us to roam freely through his domain after providing us with much valuable information, and David Junk, Ranger, who directed us to several locations; Wayne Brannan, Superintendent, Ayres Natural Bridge; Professor Dennis H. Knight, University of Wyoming; Michael A. Massie, Curator of South Pass City State Historic Site; Craig Bromley at the Bureau of Land Management in Lander, Wyoming; Corky Ramsey; G. A. Brower at Fort Hall and Leonard Carlson, head of the City of Pocatello Parks and Recreation Department; Max Newlin, Manager, Massacre Rocks State Park; Eric Bergoch, Twin Falls; and Charlie McNeil, Bruneau Dunes State Park.

We owe a big debt of gratitude to Bob and Bertha Rennells for their hospitality, for taking us over sections of the Oregon Trail, and for imparting to us a little of their extensive knowledge about the Trail; Robert C. Amdor, Superintendent, Whitman Mission National Historic Site; Frank Dixon at the Barlow National Forest Ranger Station; Sergeant Dan E. Wolf, State Police, at Government Camp; Ida Darr; the staff at the Zigzag National Forest Ranger Station; Dr. Stephen Dow Beckham, without whose help we might not have had such precise information about Laurel Hill; and Milton W. Belsher, who added to our Laurel Hill knowledge.

In the course of obtaining the photographs for this book we often had to leave established roads and highways and venture onto private land. Permission to do so was never refused. Most of the landowners allowed us free access to their lands and more than a few took the time to show us the trace of the Oregon Trail on their property. (From them we also learned a lot about barbed wire, bulls, rattlesnakes, and gate latches.) These helpful people are: Mrs. Stella Hammett; Ivor Dilky; Steve Lauer; Marion Dehning; Hubert Beal—who made us feel closer to the Oregon Trail because his grandfather had traveled over part of it; Vivian and Vern Kallsen whom we bothered perhaps more than we should have; Jolene Kaufman; and John and Albert Meyer.

We are especially indebted to Mr. and Mrs. Bernard Sun, who provided not only hospitality, but a privileged look at certain items pertaining to the Oregon Trail; Jack Corbett; and Marvin Fager and his grandchildren, Travis and Robin, who showed us some revealing aerial photographs.

Since we were "on the Trail" literally for over six months, we had to depend on a photographic lab that would work with us by mail so we could get our processing done as the film was shot. White's Color Center, Inc., in Omaha, Nebraska, provided us with this most important service. Dawn Kemp and Edith Merila at Flash Photo in Casper, Wyoming, also helped in this respect, as did Becky Basler at Quick Photo in Portland, Oregon.

After the photography was completed, we finished up our research at the Oregon Historical Society with the able assistance of Layne Woolschlager, Manuscripts Librarian, Peggy Haines, and other members of the cooperative staff.

In the states involved with the Oregon Trail, the personnel in various state and local agencies and groups has done some fine work in preserving and interpreting the Oregon Trail. We appreciate all their efforts, and especially, what has been accomplished under the direction of Eugene T. Mahoney, Director, Nebraska Game and Parks Commission.

We are glad that Greg Franzwa compiled his two excellent books: *The Oregon Trail Revisited*, and *Maps of the Oregon Trail*; they made following the Trail easy and enjoyable.

And, Ted and Pat, it was a pleasure working with you.

Permission to use excerpts from certain emigrants' writings kindly has been granted by the following: Baker County Public Library, Baker, Oregon; The Bancroft Library, University of California, Berkeley, California; The Beinecke Rare Book and Manuscript Library, Yale University, New Haven, Connecticut; Chicago Historical Society, Chicago, Illinois; The Arthur H. Clark Company, Glendale, California; Mrs. Helen Stratton Felker, Tacoma, Washington; Lane County Historical Society, Eugene, Oregon; Oregon Historical Society, Portland, Oregon; Harvey Scott Memorial Library, Pacific University, Forest Grove, Oregon; The Signal-American, Weiser, Idaho; and Utah Historical Quarterly, Salt Lake City, Utah.

PREFACE

To obtain the photographs for this book, we followed the Oregon Trail as the emigrants did, beginning in Independence, Missouri, in the spring. We traveled through Kansas, Nebraska, Wyoming, and Idaho, and arrived in the Willamette Valley, in Oregon, in the fall. The emigrants averaged about 15 miles a day but our average was somewhat slower.

Our idea was to take you, the viewer/reader, on a photographic journey along the Oregon Trail—so that you could see it, in the same chronological order and in the same seasons, as when the pioneers traversed it in the years from 1841 to 1860. In this we have been successful.

In keeping with the emigrant's point of view, we had to photograph sites and locations without the intrusion of modern elements—utility wires, paved highways, and the like. We succeeded in this, too, for the most part, but, in the process, we had to omit some important places because civilization has encroached too much. If a pertinent location is missing, it is for this reason. Unfortunately, Independence, Missouri, the beginning of the Oregon Trail, is one of those omitted. Independence Square today is a charming place in a delightful town, but it is nothing like it was in the days of the Oregon Trail, so you will find no photograph of it here.

Most of the photography was done in the many areas where the Oregon Trail, or the landmarks along it, are virtually unchanged from yesteryear. Even in these places, though, a manifestation of our twentieth century lives will occasionally intrude into a photograph. Where these occur, we hope they are unobtrusive, mild impositions and do not destroy the essence of the Trail as it was in pioneer days.

Along with our captions for the photographs will be found quotes from an emigrant's diary or journal that tells how he or she saw the scene. You will notice some inconsistencies: sometimes the diarist will have described a rushing tumbling river whereas the photograph shows a placid body of water. This is because dams now have tamed nearly all the once free-running streams. The South Platte River is much narrower—by a mile or more—than it was in the middle of the nineteenth century. Two of the greatest "tourist" attractions seen by the covered wagon travelers were the fascinating, other-worldly landscape of the Soda Springs in Idaho, and the American Falls on the Snake River. Both are now completely covered by a reservoir. Erosion, too, has taken its toll. What may have been mentioned as merely a steep descent may show in the photograph as a deeply-worn, impassable gully.

The pioneers also tended to overestimate heights: one early traveler reckoned the Wind River Mountains to have peaks over 20,000 feet high. Another calculated the Snake River chasm to be a mile deep—considerably more than its actual depth of some 400 feet at that point.

Since this book is not a verbal history of the Oregon Trail, we have taken the liberty of correcting the spelling and punctuation in some of the emigrants' quotes.

The only included original man-made structures that are connected with the Oregon Trail are the Hollenberg Ranch House near Hanover, Kansas, and some of the buildings at Fort Laramie, Wyoming. All others pictured are reconstructions. Most were rebuilt on the site of the original, but the reconstruction of Fort Hall was done in Pocatello, Idaho, several miles south of its original location on the Snake River. The ox team and wagon at Rock Creek Station State Historical Park is, of course, a re-creation and the wagon is not authentic.

Those who have not explored the Oregon Trail in depth might be surprised at how much of it actually remains. While miles and miles of it have been plowed under, or torn up for pipeline routes, or paved-over in a city, much of the old Trail exists and can be seen today. Whenever possible, we have included the actual ruts or swales in the photographs. In any picture, wherever a distinct path or road is shown, it is the Oregon Trail. Some sections of the Trail are now used as ranch roads, but they still follow in the trace of the original Trail.

The ruts show up in the photographs in a variety of ways. They may be parallel or converging lines of lighter or darker vegetation. The plant growth in the swales may be shorter or taller than in surrounding areas. Sometimes the ruts appear as fuzzy-edged straight black lines. Often there is nothing more than a depression in the earth.

Each photograph containing original ruts is noted in the directory at the back of the book. The map following the directory indicates where each photograph was taken. It includes major cities and towns and present day highway numbers to aid in locating sites, but because of space limitations, only the general area can be shown.

Should this book whet your appetite for more thorough investigation of the Oregon Trail, Chambers of Commerce and local information centers can provide detailed directions and, often, maps for more precise locating.

In the states involved, many of today's major highways follow the route of the Oregon Trail. At significant Trail sites along the way are historic markers, interpretive displays, and city, county, and state parks that all play a part in the preservation of the Oregon Trail. Most localities are proud of their association with the Trail and usually have well-marked routes to the related historic sites in their area, if they are off the main highways. Scott's Bluff, Nebraska; Fort Laramie, Wyoming; the Whitman Mission, and Fort Vancouver in Washington, all maintained by the National Park Service, are located on or near the Oregon Trail and figured significantly in the westward movement. The Visitor Centers at each have excellent informative programs. During the summer months, living history demonstrations are held regularly, which add greatly to the Oregon Trail experience.

You can take a two-week trip across the entire Oregon Trail and sample a few of its delights, or you can take months as we did, and explore it thoroughly. Since most people cannot spend months at a time on the trail, you might take your "months" in two- or three-week sections.

For serious Trail following, we recommend two extremely helpful publications: *The Oregon Trail Revisited*, and *Maps of the Oregon Trail*, both by Gregory M. Franzwa. They are available from Patrice Press in Gerald, Missouri, if they cannot be found in a bookstore. *The Oregon Trail Revisited* gives detailed directions for following nearly every one of the Trail's miles from Independence to Oregon City. Each of the maps in the map book covers an area of approximately 15 by 20 miles. They contain all roads and highways, rivers, creeks, streams, and, of course, the route of the Oregon Trail. The Trail can be followed by using just the map book, but it will not provide all the information you may need. Some sites are on private land and permission must be obtained to visit them, and some places should only by explored in a four-wheel-drive vehicle. *The Oregon Trail Revisited* provides this information. Another handy book, also from Patrice Press, is *Historic Sites Along the Oregon Trail*, by Aubrey L. Haines. This book lists, locates, and describes every site that has any connection with the Oregon Trail.

If you want to see the Oregon Trail, don't delay. The great landmarks, such as Chimney Rock and Independence Rock, will always be there, but the remnants of the Trail, the ruts and swales, are in danger of being destroyed by man or nature in many places.

Bill and Jan Moeller

THE OREGON TRAIL

Overland the pioneers came by the tens of thousands—the greatest migration in recorded history—leaving their mark forever imprinted on the face of the land.

No one knows precisely why this vast westward movement took place, for a variety of reasons contributed to it:

The West was a new and challenging frontier. The East was becoming crowded and many of those living there were beginning to feel hemmed-in by neighbors who lived a mile or two away. States such as Kentucky and Tennessee, and Missouri, at the edge of the West, had seen their populations increase two- and three-fold. Many felt that Oregon was a land that would offer them a better life, or would enable them to make their fortune. The promise of adventure was all the reason needed for some.

Pure and simple patriotism was the motivation for a great many who joined the Oregon movement. The Oregon Territory extended from the Rocky Mountains to the Pacific Ocean. It belonged to the United States because it was included in the Louisiana Purchase, but it was under England's domination by virtue of the several forts and trading posts of the Hudson's Bay Company throughout the region. England's right to be there, however, was disputed by residents of the States, politicians and farmers alike. If the United States was to claim the territory that rightfully belonged to it, it would need to have sizable numbers of its citizens settle there. It was hoped that this would be a peaceable way of wresting control from England.

Perhaps, though, it was nothing more than the pioneering instinct, ingrained into so many Americans, that drove them to expand the known frontiers. Their fathers and grandfathers had been pioneers before them and they were simply carrying on the tradition.

Most of the overlanders were bound for the Willamette Valley in Oregon, an incredibly fertile plain running in a north-south direction for nearly 100 miles. They had heard that it was sheltered from all violent weather by the Coast Range on the west and the Cascade Mountains to the east. The valley had been heralded as having no blizzards, very little snow, and a mild climate; there were no temperature extremes in winter or summer. It received copious amounts of rain, but it fell gently and was not the result of thunderstorms, hurricanes, or tornado-spawning weather. It was ideal for the agrarian emigrants.

The first who followed the trail to the West were the fur trappers who were, in turn, using established Indian trails. It was in 1812 that one of these trappers, Robert Stuart, found an easy way across the Continental Divide. Without a pass over which wagons could be taken, much of the West would not have been settled as early as it was.

It was not until 1830, however, that wheeled vehicles were taken over part of the route. In 1836, a small party lead by Dr. Marcus Whitman, a physician and missionary, successfully completed the journey to what is now Walla Walla, Washington. Other missionaries, both Catholic and

Protestant, followed. In 1842, 112 people—the first of the overlanders—left from Independence, Missouri. After that, there was no holding back the migrating tide.

Independence came to be the initial departure point for the Oregon Trail because it was the beginning of the Santa Fe Trail, which had been in use since 1823.

Most of the early emigrants arrived at Independence after traveling up the Missouri River by steamboat from St. Louis. They needed teams, wagons, and supplies before they could start for the West.

It was not long before enterprising individuals recognized that there was a good deal of money to be made from outfitting the overlanders. Soon suppliers set up shop in St. Joseph, Missouri. They advertised that it was the best place from which to leave because it was farther north and west than Independence and, so situated, it eliminated 20 miles and several river crossings.

Within a few years, wagon trains were departing from several towns along the Missouri River between St. Joseph and Council Bluffs, Iowa—then called Kanesville.

The more northern jumping-off places appealed to those coming from Illinois and Indiana; the would-be-pioneers could outfit in the towns where they lived, buying their supplies and equipment from people they knew. It would not be necessary to put their trust in traders who were apt to gouge the greenhorns.

All emigrants who left from any place south of Council Bluffs eventually followed the south side of the Platte River until it was crossed in western Nebraska. Those who departed from Council Bluffs—by 1850 they were in the majority—stayed on the north side of the Platte. The two trails usually joined at either Fort Laramie, Wyoming, or near Casper, Wyoming.

The Oregon Trail and California Trail were one in the same until they split, either at Fort Bridger, Wyoming, or Soda Springs, or the Raft River, in Idaho.

Over the years several shortcuts, or supposed shortenings of the Trail, came into, and went out of, favor. Two that eventually became a part of the main Trail were the Sublette Cutoff in Wyoming, that lopped off 100 miles by heading straight across the Little Colorado Desert to the Green River, and the Barlow Road in Oregon, which offered an overland way to Oregon City instead of the water passage down the Columbia River.

In some areas, one branch of the Trail might follow close to a river, while another might take a parallel route across a plateau. At times the pioneers, or their captains or guides, would have to decide whether it was better to go through deep sand or cross numerous creeks, or to travel through steep, hilly terrain instead of making a waterless journey across a flat desert.

On the way to Oregon and California, during the 18-year period ending in 1860, nearly 300,000 people, with some 75,000 wagons, and uncountable livestock, coursed over the various routes and left an unmistakable road—

as well defined as any modern highway. In many places the track is just as visible today.

When the pioneers started out, their wagons were brightly painted and trimmed in a contrasting color. The sparkling white covers were emblazoned with the owners' names, where they were from, and such slogans as: "On to Oregon," or, "Oregon or Bust." The American flag was prominently displayed on many wagons.

The heavy lumbering Conestoga wagon was not used on the overland trail in any great numbers; lightness was too important a factor for them to be employed successfully. The wear and tear on draft animals from pulling a load heavier than absolutely necessary had to be considered. The supplies that would be needed weighed enough without having the wagon itself compound the problem.

Guidebooks gave specifications as to how a suitable wagon should be built and outfitted. Oxen or mules were the preferred draft animals. The argument never was resolved about which were the best animals for the Trail. The choice was often made because of the cost; mules cost three times as much as oxen.

The versatile covered wagon was an ideal vehicle for overland travel, and was a comfortable cozy home. The canvas cover was of a double thickness. The outer shell was waterproofed with paint, or by oiling. Storage chests were often built to fit snugly against the inside of the wagon box; others could be lashed outside. Extra storage space was often arranged by partitioning an area under a false floor and by sewing pockets onto the inside of the cover.

The wagon tires were of iron but, to keep down the weight, iron was used in other locations only for reinforcement. The wagons could not turn at much of an angle because the big wheels extended well above the floor of the box. The lack of maneuverability was never a major problem, and it was not considered a sacrifice because the pulling was much easier than with a small-wheeled wagon.

Since there were no springs on the wagons, most people preferred to walk, or ride a horse if they had one, rather than endure the constant jolting and lurching. Ox teams were not controlled with reins, so even the driver walked alongside the plodding animals using a whip and spoken commands—and curses—when needed. The usual rate of travel was about two miles an hour, 15 miles on an average day, and it was an easy pace for both man and beast.

The pioneers became terribly attached to their animals, especially so after they had served them well for hundreds of miles. They suffered along with them through the heat, dust, and waterless grassless distances. When a weary animal would lie down in its tracks, it was heart-wrenching to have to coax it to stand up and resume its killing work. The sadness when an animal died was felt only more so when a human loved-one expired. Stalwart men were known to shed tears when a faithful animal could go on no more.

Several techniques were developed for taking wagons down hills. If the incline was not too steep, the oxen could be left hitched to the wagon to check its speed. Often the wagon's wheels were locked to further slow it.

In the few places where there were trees, ropes could be tied to the wagons, then a few turns taken around a sturdy trunk, which acted as a snubbing winch. If no trees were handy, every available person was expected to lend a hand at the ropes. On the steepest hills, where timber was plentiful, trees were tied, tops foremost, to the wagons as a drag. Usually the branches were cut close to the trunk so their short stubs would dig into the earth.

If the top-heavy wagons were to be taken across a steep slope instead of down it, ropes could be secured to the upper side of a wagon and handlers would keep a strain on the ropes as they walked alongside.

For fording rivers the methods were even more ingenious. Some emigrants simply caulked their wagon boxes, making them watertight, and floated them over. Wagons had rather high clearance and shallow water presented no problem if the boxes were raised by putting blocks on the axles; water of nearly four feet in depth could be crossed without wetting the wagon contents.

For crossing deep water eight or more teams were hitched to one wagon so that one of the teams would always be on solid ground, and would have some degree of control over those who were swimming. Unfamiliar fords were scouted by men who swam, or took a horse, across. They often carried a rope along, which was fastened on each side of the river. The rope served as a guide and helped to prevent swimming animals from being swept away by the current.

A timely departure was crucial for the well-being of the humans and animals. The overlanders could not leave too early in the spring because grass for the animals had to have time to grow. But they could not delay too long, or all the forage would have been eaten by the livestock of earlier trains. Oxen were not the only foraging animals; other cattle and sheep were driven overland—a quarter million in an average year.

The departure date could not be postponed until the grass had a chance to grow again because it would be well into the fall or early winter when the emigrants reached the Blue Mountains in eastern Oregon; they would have to cross in the snow or not be able to cross at all. No matter when the pioneers left, as the Trail became more crowded, cattle often had to be driven as much as five miles from the campground to find any grass.

In wet years, delays of many days were caused by swollen rivers and streams made unfordable by flooding. One wagon train was held up for 17 days before it could cross an insignificant stream.

Whenever they departed, whatever the year, every emigrant had to contend with drenching rain, usually hail, and winds that demolished wagons and tents—all the products of violent prairie thunderstorms. In the early spring it was often numbingly cold along with the wetness.

The overlanders reached the desert in midsummer. Their discomfort from the heat was heightened by the dust which occurred with monotonous regularity through Wyoming, Idaho, and eastern Oregon. The heavy traffic ground the earth into a fine powder that crept into every crevice and shrouded the wagons, people, and animals.

After leaving Fort Hall in Idaho, the dust was as bad, or worse, than any other place on the Oregon Trail. Many accounts tell of driving hub-deep in the stuff—and most wagon wheels were five feet in diameter. At times, the dust was so thick that the emigrants could not see their lead team from the wagon.

During the migration years, the climate was generally colder than it is now. Nearly everyone found several inches of snow on the ground at South Pass in midsummer. Many references were made to having to chop ice from ponds and water-filled containers in late spring and early fall, at places where the altitude was not enough in itself to account for this phenomenon.

Whether the emigrants were on schedule or not, snow and cold weather were often encountered in the Blue Mountains, and at the higher elevations on the Barlow Road through the Cascade Range.

Trees were common in Missouri, and groves were regularly found until the Platte River was reached. There, along its entire length where it bordered the Oregon Trail, the only timber was the skimpy willows and occasional small cottonwood growing on islands in the middle of the river; there was none on either bank.

A cluster of ash trees grew at the springs in Ash Hollow and the limestone cliffs around the hollow harbored a sparse growth of cedar. No other trees of any consequence were seen until the cedar-wooded Black Hills just west of Fort Laramie.

Once these hills were left behind, the Oregon Trail was virtually treeless until the wooded banks of the Boise River (in Boise, Idaho) were reached. Many miles from there were the Blue Mountains whose slopes were covered with magnificent pines and firs. Once reached, the pioneers could enjoy the bounty of wood for cooking fires and wagon repairs for only two or three days before they were again traveling over treeless land; no more timber was to be had until near their final destination.

Grass was abundant on the prairies although it was heavily grazed by the buffalo herds and the emigrants' livestock. Western Nebraska was the beginning of the sagebrush and it stretched endlessly across the land:

"The everlasting sage seems to have taken full possession of the country."

"Hundreds and thousands of acres with no vestige of anything but this hateful weed."

Only the pleasant green valleys of the Bear River in eastern Idaho, and the Grande Ronde River in northeastern Oregon, presented a different vista.

Finally, on the volcanic plain beyond the Blue Mountains, the sage began to disappear and gave away to a grass-like vegetation—not a refreshing green, when the overlanders arrived in this section, but golden and dry. This same sort of vegetation continued across much of Oregon until it was replaced by the damp green mosses of the Cascades and the Columbia River Gorge.

At the Oregon Trail's departure point, or shortly thereafter, a captain was chosen to lead each wagon train. He was to make the decisions regarding the security of the train, select where and when to camp, delegate scouts and night watches, and mediate disputes. The job never could be considered a permanent one, for if the other members of the train disagreed with the captain—which they did with regularity—he was voted out and replaced with another.

It was considered wise to travel in numbers for security and defense, and so that there would be enough men to stand watches all night, every night. Often the wagon trains were made up of families that had come from the same area, but companies also were formed of people who had no previous acquaintance with each other. No matter who the companies were composed of, some people eventually would split from the group and join another who did things more to their liking; not stopping to observe the Sabbath was the cause of much dissention.

In some cases a guide was hired by the members of the train. Often the guide was a mountain man who was heading west anyway. He knew the route, at least as far as the Rocky Mountains. He had knowledge about the Indians and how they should be handled, and he was invariably a better shot than any of the overlanders, so would be able to supplement their diet with game.

No matter how carefully they planned, the emigrants found that soon after starting out, they had to lighten their loads. Even on the level prairie the weight of the loaded wagons was too much for the teams to pull, or it would cause the wagon axles to snap.

Later on, as the Trail began to climb in altitude through more difficult terrain, the wagons had to be lightened even more. And the process continued until far into what is now Oregon. When teams were too weak to pull the wagon, or when it broke down where repairs could not be made, the wagon itself was abandoned.

Everything that was discarded was left alongside the Trail. The overlanders could not give things away because everyone in the train was faced with the same problem.

Along one stretch, a traveler wrote of seeing thousands of dollars worth of furniture, stoves, and equipment, heaped up on either side of the Trail, like a much-elongated, well-stocked general store.

Cast iron stoves were usually the first things to go, but eventually cherished heirlooms and treasured possessions had to be indiscriminately left to go to ruin.

Where there was no wood to be had, the precious furniture was used as fuel. Any wagons that were disabled beyond repair were used as firewood.

Cooking proved to be no problem, even without a stove, or wood for fuel. A fire pit—a narrow trench in the earth, about a foot deep and two or three feet long—served remarkably well for the task. Unless the cook had a few metal rods to lay across the top of the trench, to form a grate, the opening was made slightly smaller than the width of the smallest pot and the cooking utensil rested on the edges of the trench.

On the treeless prairie there was an excellent source of fuel provided by the millions of buffalo that roamed the area. Buffalo chips—dried dung—burned with very little odor and made a hot fire. At first, when a pioneer woman had to gather the chips in her apron, it was looked upon as a disagreeable task, but it soon became second nature and was accepted as a routine part of trail life.

The buffalo provided the emigrants with plenty of fresh meat until they passed out of their range. The animals roved over the plains in herds of hundreds and thousands. Sometimes the plains were black with the great beasts as far as the eye could see.

Because of the density of the buffalo herds it was easy for even an inexpert shot to bring one down. Buffalo hunting was a great sport among the emigrants and engaged in as much for the fun of it as for providing food.

Many of the overlanders witnessed buffalo stampedes and never forgot the sight, the sound, or the awesome feeling it engendered, as long as they lived.

Antelope was another abundant food source, but it took a good marksman to hit one of the fleet animals. Jack rabbits, deer, mountain sheep, ducks, sage hens, and grouse were also used for food. Fish abounded in most of the rivers and streams—one was described as being thick with trout—and welcome fresh salmon were plentiful in western Idaho along the Snake River.

The guidebooks recommended provisioning with certain foodstuffs: such staples as flour, sugar, dried beans and fruit, corn meal, and rice. During the summer months the emigrants' diet was supplemented with greens and wild berries picked along the way. Milk cows were taken along by many of the overlanders and as long as there was fresh milk, there was also fresh butter; milk was put into a suitable container and churned by the constant jolting of the wagon. Saleratus—baking soda—could be found in quantity around the edges of some alkali ponds.

Initially the journey from Independence to the Willamette Valley took anywhere from five to six months. As the Oregon Trail became more heavily used, ferries and bridges sprang up at river crossings, and more trading posts and forts were built. These establishments helped to shorten the travel time by as much as a month: no longer were the emigrants held up at the rivers because of high water, repairs could be made quickly and conveniently, and most important, trail-worn draft animals could be traded for fresh ones, thus avoiding long layovers to rest the teams.

A toll was charged for the use of each bridge and ferry, and it was a lucrative business for the operator of the facility. Seeing how a quick profit could be made, some wily overlanders halted their own journey long enough to slap together some kind of a raft to serve as a ferry boat and collect their own fees.

The charges for ferriage ranged from one to eight dollars. Many emigrants thought this was exorbitant and, rather than pay, chose to ford the river. Some ferry operators took exception to this and tried to dissuade them at gunpoint. There are a few recorded incidents of pioneers or ferry operators being killed in these confrontations.

It was not only at the river crossings that the overlanders were rankled. They considered the prices for supplies at the trading posts too high. Most held a low opinion of the traders and felt they were concerned with lining their own pockets more than anything else. Many were.

There were also mobile entrepreneurs, with goods-laden wagons, who traveled along with the emigrants' trains, ready to supply them with whatever they needed— as long as there was cold cash to pay for it.

The Oregon Trail held its share of terrors, one of which was the Elephant.

Many of the emigrants started out with trepidation and apprehension. From guidebooks and newspaper accounts written by pioneers who had made the trip, they knew of things that could cause problems along the way: cholera or other diseases could strike, rivers would have to be forded, the dreaded pass through the Rocky Mountains would have to be negotiated, or they might suffer from cold, wet, hunger, or the death of loved ones.

If these things, singly or combined, happened to the pioneers to the point where they felt they could not bear up under it, or did not want to go on, it was said that they had seen the Elephant. If someone saw too much of the mythical beast that supposedly ranged far and wide over the West, it was often the cause of abandoning the whole venture and turning back. The Elephant was not real, but the things it stood for were.

When the potential emigrants were planning or contemplating the overland journey from their comfortable safe farms, villages, and towns, the possibility of meeting hostile Indians was one of their greatest concerns. They all expected to have some sort of confrontation with them and worried about coming through unscathed or unscalped.

Generally, however, the Indians were no problem; they were, instead, helpful and cheerfully friendly. Many Indians provided—for a price—services or supplies needed by the pioneers. They operated ferries, helped drive stock across rivers, and rounded up cattle that had wandered away from campsites. Some Indian women had thriving businesses of supplying moccasins to emigrants whose shoes had worn out; sooner or later this happened to all of them.

The overlanders engaged in trading with nearly all the tribes they encountered along the Trail. A red shirt, or other piece of clothing, was often exchanged for fresh salmon along the Snake River. A trinket or food might be offered for some simple service performed. When an emigrant's horse was worn out, the Indians could be counted on to have others to trade for. Where horses were concerned, though, the whites nearly always got the worst of the deal.

Death was a constant companion on the Oregon Trail, but it was not because of Indians. Of the nearly 300,000 who began an overland migration, fewer than 400 died as a result of Indian attacks. It must be said that in the period between 1840 and 1850, many of the Indian incidents were precipitated by whites. Almost universally they felt they were superior to the Indians. This attitude, coupled with a lack of knowledge about them, their customs and habits, caused most of the trouble. Often an imagined social slight, a harmless prank, or some unintentional misbehavior, was enough cause for an Indian to be shot.

Some emigrants started out with the aim to "get me an Injun," and wantonly murdered one, or more, at the first opportunity. This brought retaliation from the Indians, though it was not often against the wagon train of the perpetrator, but against the next train the Indians encountered. These seemingly random Indian attacks fired the whites' hatred and, in turn, caused more retaliatory killings.

The number of deaths from causes other than Indians is estimated to be about 15,000. Disease killed more people than anything else and accounted for nine out of 10 deaths. Often less than a week had gone by, after leaving Independence, before a burial was held. A wagon train that made it all the way to Oregon without losing one of its party was luckier than most.

Asiatic cholera claimed the most lives. It was not contagious but contracted from drinking polluted water. Hundreds succumbed to the disease. It could kill its victims within hours after the first symptoms appeared. There was no known treatment. Either the victims died, or they did not, for some survived after being deathly ill for a few days.

Accidents caused a great number of deaths. Many wagon trains were traveling arsenals. The emigrants had armed themselves to be prepared for, mainly, Indian attacks and to shoot game that might be needed to augment their food supply. Most of them knew little or nothing about firearms and probably could not have hit a moving, or unmoving, target in a critical situation. Many persisted in removing their guns, by the barrel, from where they were kept. Serious wounds and death often resulted from this mishandling. One ill-starred fellow had managed to fire at, and hit, a wolf. In his excitement he dropped his gun. It fell against a rock, which caused it to discharge, putting a bullet through his heart.

Wagon accidents were quite common. Many children, especially, were killed or maimed when they jumped down from the moving wagon and fell under the wheels.

Drownings at river fords also took their toll. And humans and animals were killed during frequent cattle stampedes.

Cecilia Emily McMillen Adams faithfully recorded what she saw as she traveled to Oregon in 1852:

June 18, Passed 21 new made graves today. It makes it seem very gloomy to us to see so many of the emigrants buried on the plains.

June 19, Passed 13 graves today.

June 20, Passed 10 graves.

June 22, Passed 7 graves. If we should go by all the camping grounds, we should see five times as many graves as we do now.

June 23, Passed 21 graves.

There were very few marked graves along the Oregon Trail. Many times the departed was buried hurriedly, with scarcely any amenities, so the train would not be held up. There was no time to fabricate even a simple marker. But when Susan Hail died, her devoted husband could not bear the thought of her resting in an unmarked grave and went back to St. Joseph to have a proper stone carved. He transported it to the grave site—a distance of over 200 miles—in a wheelbarrow.

It was erroneously believed that Indians would dig up graves for the deceaseds' clothing. For this reason, and to prevent wolves from unearthing the remains, when there was time, some of the dead were interred in the Trail.

The wagons were rolled over the grave to tamp down the earth and leave no evidence that anyone had been buried there.

As the emigrants neared the end of the Oregon Trail, great numbers of them had run out of provisions and were starving. Others were exhausted and sick. Many were destitute; they had lost their wagons and belongings, or used up their funds in paying tolls and ferry charges.

It was common for established Oregon residents to mount relief expeditions to aid those just arriving. Concerned and charitable settlers regularly took pack trains from the Dalles to intercept companies of overlanders to help them along the final miles and do what they could to ease their suffering.

Whether the emigrants traversed the Oregon Trail with no problems or an abundance of them, the overland journey was the most significant experience of their lives. It affected the lives of the thousands yet to come, for the pioneers opened the way that led to the settlement of the West. They who established and defined the Oregon Trail were those who molded and unified the country. Because of them, the United States reaches contiguously from ocean to ocean.

Two main branches of the Oregon Trail led from Independence, Missouri. The southernmost followed the established Santa Fe Trail.

On each branch, just a few miles from the departure point, the untried oxen, their inexperienced drivers, the excited children, and apprehensive women, crossed their first river, the Blue, and made their initial pull up the sloping embankment on the other side—the beginning of their seasoning for the long road that lay ahead.

Crossed the Blue soon in the morning.
Virgil Pringle, May 8, 1846

I made a very thorough examination of the Blue Mound and,
if it had not been such an immense mass, should have left
it believing that it was the work of man.

John Minto, June, 1844

Appearing strangely out of place, Blue Mound rose out of the flat land around it like a giant swelling. Coming upon it was an occasion even though it was only a few days from Independence; it was the first distinct height of land the pioneers saw.

An epidemic of Asiatic cholera killed at least 50 emigrants who were camped near the Red Vermillion River crossing. Perhaps a descendant of another tree that grew here over 100 years ago, this giant elm, a foot short of 100 feet tall, is a magnificent memorial for the victims buried here, most in unmarked graves.

A toll bridge, in existence in 1848, and owned by Louis Vieux, a Potawatomi Indian chief, was used by some overlanders to cross this small river with its sharply angled banks.

The Vermillion is the worst stream we have crossed, the banks
are so steep and muddy and rocky.

Rebecca Ketcham, 1853

After Edwin Bryant named the place, George M. McKinstry carved the name in eight-inch high letters on a large flat stone above the spring's runoff. Not a few others incised their names into the limestone; among them was James F. Reed, who later was to be one of the survivors of the ill-fated Donner party.

The spring hollow was heavily and variously timbered with oaks, cottonwoods, walnuts, and sycamores. When most of the wagon trains arrived, the trees were greening with the delicate colors of spring, the grass was lush and plentiful, and wildflowers blossomed everywhere. Lovely as it was, this site, only a few days' journey from Independence, carried its burden of sorrow. On the heights around it, safe from any flooding, were the graves of many who had already succumbed to cholera.

In 1846, when the family of Sarah Keyes set off westward, the plucky 70-year-old woman steadfastly refused to be left behind in Illinois. Even though her health was failing, she was determined to travel with her daughter as far as she could. Her final resting place is beneath a large oak on a hillock above Alcove Spring.

...a most beautiful spring and a fall of water of 12 feet.

George M. McKinstry, May 30, 1846

The Hollenberg Ranch house was built on the Oregon Trail in 1857 near the junction with the trail from St. Joseph, Missouri. It was used as a trading post and later served as a Pony Express station. Though few in number, houses and other structures were not an uncommon sight in the beginning miles of the Oregon Trail but farther on, when such an ordinary thing as a house was seen again, usually far into the Oregon Territory, it was invariably commented on by the pioneers.

By the time the emigrants reached Rock Creek they were truly on the prairie. They could see for miles in all directions from the low brows of the gently undulating hills. This was the landscape that evoked the many references to the sea found in the emigrants' writings.

Imagine the ocean, when the waves are rolling mountains high, becoming solid and covered with beautiful green grass and you have some faint idea of it.

Rebecca Ketcham, May, 1853

Perhaps this is one of the most remarkable rivers in the world. Like the Nile it runs hundreds of miles through a sandy desert. The valley of this stream is from fifteen to twenty miles wide, a smooth level plain, and the river generally runs in the middle of it, from west to east. The course of this stream is more uniform than any I have ever seen. It scarcely ever makes a bend. This river has low, sandy banks, with sandy bottom, and the water is muddy.

Peter H. Burnett, 1853

The Platte River, east of the forking of its northern and southern branches, was unlike any river the overlanders had ever seen; it was randomly wide and narrow, shallow and deep—but mostly shallow, liberally sprinkled with stagnant pools, mudflats, and sandbars, and always, unvaryingly, muddy. The Platte was the subject of much ridicule: "too thick to drink and too thin to plow," "a mile wide and a foot deep," "the river that flowed upside down." One diarist wrote: "encamped on the bank (if it has a bank) of the far famed Platte River." Yet this derided body of water washed the shores of what was known as the Coast of Nebraska.

Fort Kearny was the first fort built solely for the protection of the ever-swelling tide of westward-bound pioneers. The unfortified outpost was completed in 1848, the same year that cottonwood trees, still standing, were planted on the parade ground.

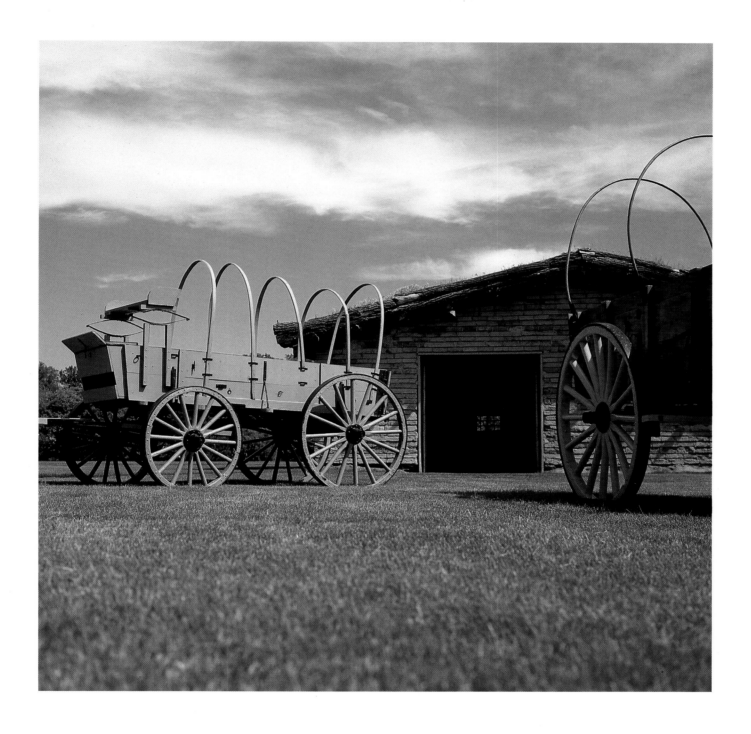

At present it consists of a number of long, low buildings constructed principally of adobe, or sun dried bricks, with nearly flat roofs of brush.

A. J. McCall, May 29, 1849

The Oregon Trail followed closely along the south side of the Platte River. At O'Fallon's Bluff the river elbowed its way around the base of the hill leaving no room for wagons. They had to be taken up and over the bluff where their wheels cut deep swales that could never be washed away by a flooding river.

On one occasion today we had to retreat over the bluff on account of the river.
Henry Allyn, June 9, 1853

Sooner or later the Platte, now called the South Platte, had to be crossed. Because of the river's width, which varied from three-quarters of a mile to a mile-and-a-half, and its ever-changing channels, it could not be successfully bridged. Because of its depth, which could be measured in inches in places, ferries could not be used.

Crossings were made variously along the length of the river as conditions and whims dictated, but the majority of the wagon trains forded the river in the vicinity of Lower California Crossing. The place got its name during the gold rush years; Upper California Crossing was some 20 miles west.

There was always apprehension because of quicksand; it was reported that the bed of the channel was entirely of quicksand, but, if it existed, it was not channel-wide and caused no serious problems. Nothing and no one was ever swallowed up by it.

We made a good forenoon drive and moved in sight of the lower crossing of the south fork of the Platte. We succeeded in crossing it. We blocked up some 10 inches, doubled teams, drove and waded, and in about three hours we got over.

John B. Spencer, June 16, 1852

After crossing the south fork of the Platte, the wagons carved many swales in the earth as they strained up the angling, nearly two-mile-long California Hill.

Had a pretty hard pull up the bluff and then found a gently rolling prairie.
James Field, June 8, 1845

There had been a few sloping river and stream banks to slow the overlander's progress, but here at Windlass Hill, was the first long steep descent of the Oregon Trail. The inviting tree-shaded Ash Hollow could be seen just ahead at the bottom of the hill. One emigrant remarked that it seemed impossible for such heavily laden wagons to descend safely, but most reached the bottom without mishap.

No record exists of any windlasses being used here, and the origin of the name is a mystery. All available men, and women, held back on ropes, tied to each wagon to slow its descent.

Here we found our first hill to go down that was worthy to be called a hill.

Andrew Jackson Wigle, 1853

Set among harsh limestone bluffs were the sylvan glade and cool springs of Ash Hollow. Here was an oasis in which to pause and linger after the adventurous plunge down Windlass Hill.

This is a beautiful place with high bluffs on all sides, there are some ash trees from which it takes its name. The greatest profusion of wild roses is in full bloom and many other flowers; the sides of the bluffs were literally covered and the air heavy with the odor of them. I was enchanted and could scarcely tear myself away.

Esther Belle Hanna, June 5, 1852

45

The Oregon Trail kept along the south side of the Platte River for about 150 miles. After the Trail crossed the high, flat, unbroken plain between Lower California Crossing and Ash Hollow, it struck the north fork of the Platte. This branch was followed for another 250 miles before the final crossing of the river was made, just before it made a great bend to the south to its distant source in the Rocky Mountains.

After the stream diverged there was little similarity between the two branches. The lethargic shallow South Platte appeared to have no connection with the North Platte, which ran full, fast, deep, and cold.

The winding Platte, the scene adorned by a setting sun, was sublime beyond description of a feeble pen.

Andrew S. McClure, June 5, 1853

Courthouse and Jail Rocks, so named because of their supposed resemblance to the architectural style of certain municipal buildings, were the first of the great formations that would be seen along the Oregon Trail. They rose majestically from the level, otherwise featureless, prairie.

Being able to see for miles was something that many of the overlanders had never experienced coming, as they did, from the wooded and forested states east of the Mississippi River. It affected their ability to correctly judge distance. They reasoned that something appearing to be so close could be reached in a few minutes. Many who attempted to attain the formations turned back after several hours because the rocks looked not much closer than they had when the emigrants started out from their campgrounds five or ten miles away.

At a distance of 15 miles it presents a very fine appearance—seeming like a great regular structure of brick with a low dome.

S. H. Taylor, June 1853

Most of the emigrants caught sight of Chimney Rock when they were two days' travel east of it—a stark solitary finger rising over 300 feet into the clear clean air above the prairie.

When approaching it, it takes a variety of forms—sometimes that of an old ruin, then a very sharp cone; but, after all, more the shape of a chimney than anything else.

A. J. McCall, June 13, 1849

During the first years of the migration west the easiest way through the towering rocks that stretched for miles, north and south, across what is now western Nebraska, was through the sweeping valley that led to Robidoux Pass.

One of the Robidoux clan, originally fur traders from St. Joseph, Missouri, operated a trading post and blacksmith shop in the valley until a better route was found through Mitchell Pass, a short distance to the north.

Good springs and grass near the trading post of a fur company.
John G. Glenn, June 27, 1852

Scott's Bluff was named for Hiram Scott, a fur trapper. He and two companions were traveling by boat down the North Platte River. Scott became ill when they were some 60 miles west of the bluff, where the three were to rendezvous with other trappers. His unfeeling comrades were sure his death was imminent, and abandoned him. Scott made his torturous way alone to the rendezvous location to find only the long-dead ashes of the trappers' campfires. There was no help for him now. He crawled to a spring at the base of the bluff where he died. His bones were found months later, after they had been picked clean by the wolves.

The unfortunate Scott's story intrigued the pioneers, and many wrote about it in great detail in their diaries.

They are beetling cliffs of indurated clay, bearing resemblance to towers, castles, and fortified cities...

A. J. McCall, June 14, 1849

The broad break in the massive sandstone and siltstone ridge of Scott's Bluff that is named Mitchell Pass, could have been called: The Gateway to the Mountains. After cresting the gentle rise of the pass, the emigrants often had their first view of what many thought were the Rockies. They were, in fact, the Laramie Mountains, and the formidable Laramie Peak, over 10,000 feet high, was visible from the pass although it was over 100 miles away.

This morning the road passed over the ridge from which we saw some of the peaks of the mountains . . .

David E. Pease, June 2, 1849

Fort Laramie was a popular place with Indians, fur trappers, and overlanders. A sizable Indian village of tipis, often numbering in the hundreds, was always in evidence around the fort. These colorful dwellings were a counterpoint to the many traditional buildings and houses that had been erected to serve the various needs of the fort.

Here supplies of all kinds could be purchased and repairs made at the blacksmith shop. Here, too, was one of the few dependable post offices along the route.

There is one two-story house very well finished at Laramie, and one large frame just raised, and several clay buildings whitewashed on the outside, which gives it quite the appearance of a village in a savage land.

Orange Gaylord, June 4, 1853

It was not ego that motivated the overlanders to inscribe their names in the many places that they did. Register Cliff, like many other places farther west, served as a message board for family and friends in following trains. An emigrant's name, and the date he or she was there, confirmed to those behind that the person had been alive on that date. It also let them know approximately how many days apart they were.

In good health, Alva H. Unthank neatly scratched his name in the soft sandstone. He was buried within days a few miles away—another victim of the quick-striking cholera.

We came along the base of a large bluff that was covered up as far as a person could reach with names and dates of those that have passed this way.

Delila Berintha Saunders, July 9, 1866

The low rough ridges west of Fort Laramie presented the most rugged terrain yet encountered. They were named the Black Hills because of the dark green cedar trees growing upon them which appeared black from a distance. Deep Rut Hill is on the western perimeter of the Black Hills.

The exposed rock atop this sandstone ridge attests to the volume of travel over the Oregon Trail more than in any other location. Year after year, as wagons by the thousands rolled over the rise, they carved their own monument to the western migration. A human hand could not have done it so well or so eloquently.

The top of the ridge is scarred with many ruts but the main track has been worn to a depth of five feet. Few emigrants remarked on what has come to be called Deep Rut Hill. During the early years of travel on the Trail, the ruts were not worn into the rock or were so commonplace that they caused no comment. It is a wonder, though, that some of the later travelers did not write about the remarkable experience of being shoulder-deep *in* the Trail.

The road through these hills is, of necessity, very circuitous; winding about as it must to avoid the steeps, ravines and rocks. We found in places a few trees of pine and cedar.

Overton Johnson and William H. Winter, 1843

Laramie Peak, the landmark that had loomed ahead for days, would soon be left behind.
The Oregon Trail never crossed the Laramie Mountains; it followed a route on the flat land along the northern curve of the range. The closest the emigrants came to Laramie Peak was 30 miles.

We are now in sight of the highest portion of earth that ever I looked upon.
William Cornell, June 24, 1852

With the Black Hills now to the east, the emigrants would spend the next few days in an area laced with pleasant easily forded streams which ensured a plentiful supply of water. There was usually good grass and even some wood for campfires.

We encamped on a most beautiful stream, called the La Bonte.
A. J. McCall, June 20, 1849

This graceful arch over La Prele Creek was two miles off the main route of the Oregon Trail. The emigrants were interested in seeing all the natural curiosities, and walking all day never dampened their enthusiasm for exploring farther once they arrived at the day's campground. If there was something to be seen, they wanted to have a look at it.

Up near the high bluff there is an arch of solid stone over this river, 40 or 50 feet wide and 15 feet high. I passed up the river, rode through beneath the arch, and viewed with delight the grand works of nature.

J. R. Starr, June 26, 1850

Just west of La Bonte Crossing the color of the earth changed from grey-brown to brick red—something new and exotic to the pioneers.

The rocks being of a reddish cast present a beautiful appearance a short distance off.

Orange Gaylord, June 7, 1853

*It is about one hundred and fifty yards long and is composed of stone piled up
on either side of the road some distance above the surface of the road, forming
a kind of pass or defile.*

Andrew S. McClure, June 27, 1853

After the North Platte River was crossed, just east of Rock Avenue, the sagebrush-covered country began in earnest. In the "avenue" jagged, lichen-decorated, sandstone slabs were tumbled helter-skelter on either side of a smooth level area just wide enough for one wagon to pass through.

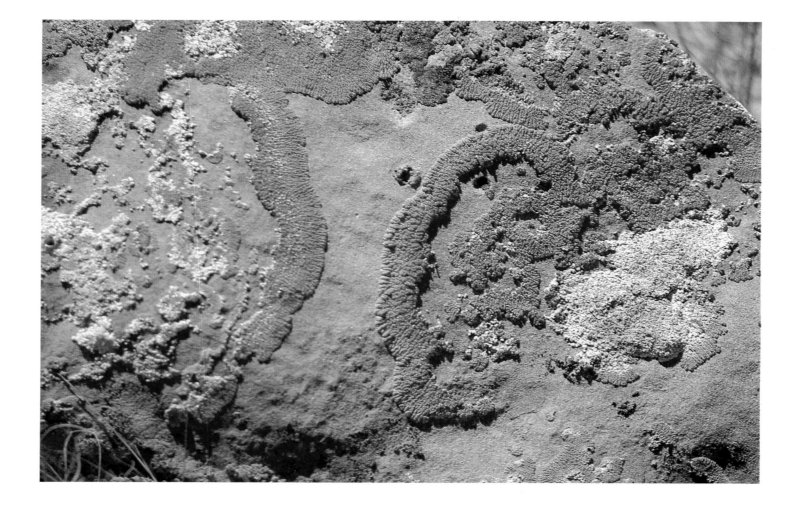

This land was not designed for subsistence of animals; there was little forage and even less drinkable water. Ponds, pools, and springs lined this part of the route, but the thirsty beasts had to be kept away from them at all costs. To drink of the alkali water meant certain death, as whitening bones of cattle around the ponds testified.

These are very poisonous and a great many cattle died from its effects. We did not let our cattle taste it, fearing its consequences. Passing on from here we saw a great many cattle lying dead and a great many that had been left which were yet alive.

J. R. Starr, July 1, 1850

At last, here in the wastes of sagebrush and alkali, the cattle could be allowed to drink to their hearts' content from the never-ending supply of cool pure water, and feast upon the sweet grass found in plentitude around Willow Spring.

We found a beautiful spring, of very cold clear water, rising in a little green valley, through which its water flowed about one mile.

Overton Johnson and William H. Winter, July 25, 1843

There is at least a million names of emigrants on the rock, some are in small type and some very large.

William Kahler, July 6, 1852

When an American Fur Company expedition found themselves at this rounded granite behemoth of a rock on the fourth of July in 1830, they decided to name it in honor of the occasion, Independence Day, hence Independence Rock.

The area around the rock was a favorite campground. The gentle meandering Sweetwater River, with an abundance of grass growing alongside it, flowed around the south side of the rock. Of the many names on the top and around the base of the rock, only those that were carved or etched into the tough stone survive.

Within sight of Independence Rock was another source of wonderment to the emigrants—Devil's Gate. The Sweetwater River runs through the shadowed declivity. Ever the tourists, many felt compelled to scramble to the top of the rocks for the view. Some even inched their way to the very edge of the rift and peered straight down onto the river nearly 400 feet below.

Everybody must take a look at it. Here the waters of the Sweetwater rush and foam through a narrow passage two hundred feet below and it takes strong nerves to look down into the rushing waters.

George Miller West, 1852

Wagons could be taken through this area on three routes, two of which were through deep sand. Considered the least difficult was to follow the Sweetwater through the rocks. The river filled the defile so that scarcely anything that could have been called a bank existed on either side. This necessitated zigzagging through the passage and, in so doing, three crossings of the river were made.

Today we have crossed the Sweetwater River three times, there being scarce a mile-and-a-half between the first and last crossing. The rocks came so near the river, first on one side, then on the other, we were obliged to cross to get along.

Rebecca Ketcham, July, 1853

Ice Slough, a shallow basin, at an altitude of 6,000 feet, held an assortment of ponds and springs. Some sections were covered over with a thick insulating layer of turf which preserved the ice that had formed in the winter. Here was another curiosity—a most welcome one—the emigrants came upon as they passed this way during the hottest months of the year.

We dug in the earth about 12 inches, and found chinks of ice. We carried it along till about noon, and made some lemonade for dinner. It relished first rate.

George Belshaw, July 4, 1853

South Pass—the crossing of the Continental Divide, the eastern boundary of the Oregon Territory, yet only the halfway point on the Oregon Trail.

The emigrants had heard of this easy pass through the Rocky Mountains but most of them imagined it to be a narrow defile, as were many other passes. How could it be otherwise in the heart of the Rockies? Nothing prepared them for the astounding nearly flat plain, stretching for miles in all directions, that, here, was the top of the continent. It looked no different from the hundreds of miles of sagebrush-covered desert they had been traversing. Yet here they were, at an altitude of 7,000 feet, after having climbed steadily, imperceptibly, ever since leaving Independence.

To the south were the low-lying Oregon Buttes, neither spectacular in height nor configuration. They resembled other similar formations the emigrants had periodically encountered beginning as far back as Scott's Bluff. A glance northward, however, to the myriad white-capped lofty peaks of the Wind River Range, looming large even though some 20 miles away, erased any doubt anyone might have had about their whereabouts.

This was confirmed by the weather at this point where the earth appeared to meet the sky. It was the rare company of pioneers that did not experience bitter night cold at the Pacific Springs campground just west of the pass, or escape the violent storms that rolled across the heights with thunder shaking the very earth, and crackling shards of lightning that seemed to rend the heavens asunder before pelting the hapless travelers with rain, hail, sleet, or snow.

We began to ascend a very gradual elevation until we reach a broad and naked plain with high, rugged, cold, blue mountain peaks to the right. The ascent is so gradual that it was difficult to fix the culminating point.
A. J. McCall, July 5, 1849

The remarkable colorful formation of Plume Rocks stands alone in the landscape. It is the only one of its kind for miles around. Although shaped by the elements, it looks as if it might have been sculpted by an artisan and placed here to be set off against the backdrop of the Wind River Mountains.

The rocks, which are not rocks at all but a conglomerate of clay and pebbles, were the last landmark of any significance the emigrants, using the Sublette Cutoff, would see until they reached the Green River. Even the towering Wind River Mountains would recede into the distance well before they reached the river.

. . .on our right, about 300 yards distant, some low clay bluffs, of a dark dingy red hue, and singularly plume-formed projections on top. . .

J. Goldsborough Bruff, August 3, 1849

By the time the Big Sandy River was reached, humans and animals alike were feeling the ravages of the journey. The overlanders were tired and the animals were weak. To reach the Green River they faced a 50-mile trek across the most desolate hostile land they had encountered thus far.

Water from the Big Sandy was stored in every available container. As much grass as could be found was gathered to feed the animals, for upon the treeless barren land was no water, no grass, no shade—only an endless plain of sagebrush with the slender ribbon of the Trail reaching ahead to infinity unless it was blotted out by the thick choking dust that was ever present when the wagons were moving.

It was more than many could tolerate to traverse these desert miles in the intense heat of the day, and many trains made the crossing at night. Even so, animals died by the score, and the emigrants were weary beyond imagining when the Green was reached. Many expected to see the Elephant on this stretch, and many did.

We take what is known as Sublette's Cutoff and at Big Sandy camp and rest making preparations to across the desert . . . a dry sandy plain without grass or water. We break camp at two A.M. and commence this dry journey.

George Miller West, June, 1852

My companions pronounce this as the most God-forsaken country they ever saw. Destitute
of timber, of grass, of game—even water scarce. They cannot see for what purpose it was

A. J. McCall, July 9, 1849

The unchanging desolate landscape stretched ahead mile after dreary mile.
To avoid traveling in a cloud of dust, which the wagons raised as they crunched over the dry earth,
the trains spread out and the wagons traveled alongside one another. The line they formed was sometimes
over a mile wide.

The Green River roiled and rumbled its way southward from its birthplace in the high snowy mountains to the north. It was a dangerous and difficult crossing. In the early years of the Trail, before a ferry was established, the river had to be forded—there was no other choice.

Unless the river was reached before the snowmelt flooding in the spring, or late in the summer when the high water had subsided, which was never the case with the overlanders, the only safe crossing was on a narrow submerged invisible gravel bar. If the course was altered by just a few feet, it often meant disaster for people, wagons, and livestock.

. . .a cold swift mountain stream, 18 rods wide. Tumbles and rolls through the mountains like a milltail.

George Belshaw, July 19, 1853

Standing alone on the desert was the singular formation known as Church Buttes. Its green and grey sandstone had been carved by the wind and weather. The resultant fantastic and grotesque shapes suggested different things to each observer.

. . .the shape of a large temple and decorated with all kinds of images: gods, and goddesses, everything that has been the subject of the sculptor: all kinds of animals and creeping things. . .

John Boardman, August 12, 1843

In early Trail days Fort Bridger was not a military fort; it was the grandiose name given to the palisaded trading post and blacksmith shop owned by Jim Bridger and Louis Vasquez.

The fort was built in a lovely well-watered valley with the snow-covered peaks of the Uinta Mountains to the south. It was opportunely situated to capitalize on trade with the overlanders and their everlasting need for a blacksmith's services.

Before the Sublette Cutoff was used, the Oregon Trail veered southwest from South Pass to a point on Black's Fork of the Green River. It then angled off to the northwest until reaching the Bear River Divide. The fort was located at the point of this large shallow irregular vee.

This is a pretty place to see in such a barren country. Perhaps there is a thousand acres of level land covered with grass interspersed with beautiful strong brooks and plenty of timber.

Elizabeth Dixon Smith, August 9, 1850

Muddy Fork, a beautiful, clear stream, with plenty of good grass on its banks.

Samuel Handsacker, July 14, 1853

Once Muddy Creek was crossed—sometimes a difficult ford because of its considerable volume of snowmelt water—the emigrants had a short respite from the sagebrush and heat of the desert as they traveled over the Bear Mountains. The track was rugged here, and steep, but not so much that they could not enjoy the change in scenery.

The emigrants, most of whom were farmers, beheld the Bear River Valley as a paradise. If it had not been so far from other settlements, some would have made it the end of the trail and established themselves there to farm its fertile soil, joining the friendly ebullient Shoshone Indians who lived happily along the river.

The basin spread before the overlanders as they came down from the heights of the Bear Mountains—an emerald green jewel in a blue mountain setting. Lush grass grew everywhere, nurtured by the Bear River that wandered extravagantly through the valley.

The trail-weary pioneers tarried here to rest themselves and to make repairs to the wagons, to catch up on household tasks, and to partake of the bounty of the place; it provided wild berries and abundant game.

Here we found pure water, sufficient for all of us and our cattle. Here we also found oceans of grass and thousands of acres of rich, level land covered with wild flax.

P. V. Crawford, July 8, 1851

The water oozed from between the rocks, the surface of which was red as blood.
Lucia Loraine Williams, July 5, 1851

Soda Springs was undoubtedly the greatest curiosity on the entire Oregon Trail. The emigrants had time to sightsee, marvel at its wonders, and sample its many-flavored waters, because they were still traveling through the hospitable Bear River Valley with nothing to concern them for at least a few miles more. They could relax and enjoy the novelty.

In an otherworldly landscape of cones and craters formed by mineral deposits were hot springs, warm springs, and cold springs, springs that tasted like soda water, others that had a metallic flavor, and one whose taste was likened to beer. The most captivating was Steamboat Spring which regularly gave off the sound of a steamboat's whistle as it gurgled, chuffed, and then exploded from its cone in a steaming geyser three feet high.

The areas around the springs were variously colored white, grey, buff, or red.

One minister, who evidently looked askance at the frolicking of his companions, said, gloomily, as he surveyed the landscape: ''Hell is not more than a mile from this place.''

West of Soda Springs the landscape changed dramatically. Here began the ancient lava fields which the Oregon Trail would continue across for the rest of its distance. The only rock on the Trail from here on, whether it was underlying the vegetation, exposing itself in ragged black outcroppings or deeply cleft sheer-sided rifts, or rising in towering mountain peaks, would be of volcanic origin.

This valley appears to have been sunk several feet and is full of chasms, from two to twenty feet wide, and of unknown depth. Volcanic rock is scattered over it, in large masses; and in many places it appears to have been upheaved from beneath. We passed on the left, a large, hollow mound, the crater of an extinguished volcano.

Overton Johnson and William H. Winter, September, 1843

The overlanders could see the white adobe walls of Fort Hall, set as it was on the flat plain near the Snake River, from five miles away. It was an outpost of the Hudson's Bay Company. Supplies, brought to Fort Hall from Astoria on the coast, could be purchased at what most considered to be exorbitant prices.

Eighteen miles today took us to Fort Hall which stands upon the level bottom of Snake River with a fine pasturage and some timber around it. It is a good-sized fort, built like Fort Laramie of unburnt brick.

James Field, July 3, 1845

Black and jagged upthrust rocks punctuated the landscape and determined the Oregon Trail's route through this area. Here it passed narrowly between rough high lava outcroppings.

Wagon trains traveled through here for nearly twenty years without any interference from the Shoshone Indians. But in 1862, Indians waited among the concealing rocks close by and set upon the unsuspecting emigrants in five separate small wagon trains. Ten were killed and as many wounded. The wagons were looted and the stock run off.

Then we marched on about eight miles and came to a rock gap that the road passed through just wide enough for wagons...

Absalom B. Harden, July 28, 1847

Although there was plenty of water to be had in the Snake River, reaching it was often impossible because of the river's precipitous, sometimes vertical, cliffs.

The river is generally difficult of access being shut in on either side with high bluffs of basaltic rock.

J. M. Harrison, 1846

As if to make up for the austerity and sameness of its valley, the Snake River was graced with myriad waterfalls. The emigrants saw some of the impressive cataracts but heard only the thunderous roar of others, when the trace of the Oregon Trail was a few miles away.

...produces a rumbling that may be heard several miles during the stillness of the night. The noise of the falls sounds like music in the ears of the lover of adventure.

Andrew S. McClure, July 27, 1853

Shallow Rock Creek, a mere 20 feet wide, flowed at the bottom of a chasm. There was only one place where the steep walls were low enough for wagons to be taken down—an eight-mile detour from the Oregon Trail's general direction.

Poor camp and you have to drive cattle down a bluff to get water;
you have to bring your using-water over a half-mile up the bluffs.

Absalom B. Harden, July, 1847

The alien volcanic land produced some scenic wonders for the emigrants' eyes to feast upon. At Thousand Springs, remarkable cascades of quicksilver water burst forth from the middle of the basalt cliffs.

Fine scenery on the opposite side of the river, rocks six or eight hundred feet high, fourteen distinct waterfalls pouring out from them, *only two coming over the top.*

Rebecca Ketcham, August, 1853

At last the Snake River escaped from the deep fissure that had sliced through the land for nearly 200 miles. The hill above the river was no longer of unassailable sheer volcanic rock but a sagebrush-covered slope that could be negotiated without too much difficulty by the teams.

n coming down to the river bottom, there s a very steep hill.

Joel Palmer, August 23, 1845

The Snake River ran between solid rock walls for most of its length so its waters picked up little sediment; they were clear—the first river of its type most of he emigrants had ever seen.

The Snake was generally six to eight feet deep at Three Island Crossing but, because of its clarity, it appeared to be quite shallow. The deceptiveness of the water's depth, coupled with the swift current, made this one of the more treacherous river crossings. Detailed instructions were given in guidebooks so as to avoid mishaps. nevertheless, drownings of men and animals occurred frequently and loaded wagons often capsized.

First we drive over a part of the river 100 yards wide to an island, then over another branch 75 yards wide to a second island; then we tied a string of wagons together by a chain...we carried as many as 15 wagons at one time. The water was 10 inches up the wagons' beds in the deeper places. It was about 9000 yards across.

William T. Newby, September 11, 1843

Those who could not, or would not, ford the Snake River at Three Island Crossing, continued along the south bank of the river and encountered a desert area the like of which paled against the so-called Great American Desert they had already traversed. Here was hub-deep sand, searing heat, and dry vegetation—what there was of it—shimmering in the heat waves. And here were tremendous sand dunes.

Fortunately the overlanders did not have to cross the dunes; they saw them rising a short distance to the south of the Oregon Trail and it gave them something, at least, to be thankful for in this bleak parched land.

The most desolate country in the whole world. The region of the shadow of death.

Samuel James, July 24, 1850

Cattle died by the thousands on the desert wastes. Already weak, the stretches without adequate food or water did them in. Instances have been noted where the wagons rolled between banks of rotting stinking carcasses. One woman wrote of holding a handkerchief to her nose but it did not keep out the stench. Another complained that the campground was intolerable because of the many dead animals lying nearby.

If they did not collapse on the way, the cattle that had survived this far could refresh themselves on the grass in a heavily wooded area a few miles ahead, and below, on the Boise River.

We found a gap in the bluffs of Boise Valley, where we turned down and succeeded in reaching the valley in safety although our road was very steep and stony and long.

P. V. Crawford, August 6, 1851

The wagons dropped off the abrupt edge of a small hill just before crossing the easily-forded Boise River at its base.

A small adobe outpost of the Hudson's Bay Company stood on the eastern bank of the Snake River near where it began its great sweep to the north to join the Columbia. Supplies could be obtained here and a ferry service was available.

The river was wide, but of a nearly uniform depth, and the current was sluggish enough so that it presented no problem to those who preferred to ford the river rather than pay ferry charges.

Crossed Snake at Fort Boise, that world renowned spot of one miserable block house all going to decay, this morning. Had no trouble in swimming the cattle.

Charlotte Stearns Pengra, August 13, 1853

After crossing the Snake River, where there was, at least, a little greenery to refresh the eye, the Oregon Trail again struck off through dry, treeless terrain.

Though it is now August, "dog days"...here it is quite cold and "winter is coming." The weeds are as dry and brown as they are in Illinois quite late in the fall.

Elizabeth Wood, August 3, 1851

The emigrants had kept uneasy company with the Snake River for most of the preceding 300 miles. Now, at Farewell Bend, they would, in the words of one diarist, "bid hur a due forever." The next major river most of them would see was the mighty Columbia itself.

Came to Snake River for the last time. Here it runs between lofty and inac- ble mountains. So farewell Snake.

Cecilia Emily McMillen Adams, August 24, 1852

A very deep narrow wooded valley all along between high mountains...much dreaded.

Samuel James, August 2, 1850

The overlanders entered the deep confined Burnt River canyon where never before had they been hemmed in by such precipitous high hills. The bottom of the canyon, through which the river flowed, was so narrow that the wagons and cattle had to be led carefully over precarious trails that had been worn on the face of the steep hillsides.

A great bowl of a valley greeted the emigrants' eyes as they edged down Ladd Canyon Hill. The incline was covered with treacherous loose slippery volcanic rock but a tree stood conveniently at hand and was put to good use for lowering the wagons. Near the bottom, as the pioneers moved sideways across the slope, and where it was not so steep, they could better appreciate the valley before them.

Came in sight of the Grande Ronde, a beautiful level valley...but O the getting down to it over a long steep and stony hill is equal to any getting downstairs I ever saw, and I have seen some on this road.

Cecilia Emily McMillen Adams, September 2, 1852

The Oregon Trail wended its way up and out of the lovely Grande Ronde Valley to cross the heavily timbered, sharply sloping Blue Mountains. The way up the mountains was no less steep than the way down.

It was here that the emigrants saw their first of the great conifer forests of the Northwest; the size of the 200-foot tall trees and the dense growth astonished them. To those overlanders who had come from the eastern states, the familiar trees brought a pang of homesickness as they remembered the pine-clad hills they had left behind.

Worst hill to go down that we have found yet, long, steep and rocky. Our road today has been mostly through lofty pines as fine as I ever saw.

Cecilia Emily McMillen Adams, September 3, 1852

Once down the first steep slope of the Blue Mountains the Oregon Trail crossed the flashing waters of the Grande Ronde River which burbled through a pleasant valley.

The stream is about fifty feet wide, with clear water running over a nice pebbly bottom.
The valley is very narrow, being only about sufficient for a wagon roadbed.

P. V. Crawford, August 21, 1851

At the top of the western edge of the Blue Mountains the pioneers could see the Cascade Range over 150 miles away—the only real remaining barrier between them and their new home. Mount Hood, Mount Saint Helens, and Mount Adams distinctly rose to their great heights above the lower-lying lesser mountains of the range.

From the brow of the mountain we had a fine view of the Cascade Range.

Overton Johnson and William H. Winter, 1843

The slow rugged way over the Blue Mountains came to an end when the wagons went down the long slope of Emigrant Hill into the Umatilla River Valley, its vegetation now in its tawny autumn color.

At last came in sight of the valley, covered entirely with dry grass. Commenced the descent...very gradual. Said to be five miles downhill. Don't think it was much overrated.
Cecilia Emily McMillen Adams, October 8, 1852

The Whitman Mission was founded in 1836 by Dr. Marcus Whitman and his charming wife, Narcissa, who, with another missionary's wife, were the first white women to cross the continent.

The Oregon Trail passed some 20 miles south of the mission but thousands of overlanders detoured to the place in the years from 1843 to 1847. Dr. Whitman took care of the sick, and provided supplies, and sometimes shelter to those who had started too late to get across the Cascades before the winter set in.

On November 29, 1847, the Cayuse Indians attacked the mission. The Whitmans were killed, along with 12 others. All the mission buildings were burned to the ground and never rebuilt.

The buildings are of unburnt brick, and are neatly and comfortably furnished. The missionaries have a mill, and cultivate a small piece of ground.

Overton Johnson and William H. Winter, 1843

Had to camp at a mud hole spring called the Well Spring. Think it is a pretty sick one myself, at least we had to carry out about two wagon loads of mud before we could get water enough for cooking purposes.

John Tully Kerns, September 10, 1852

Here in the empty sere land west of the Umatilla River was the only source of water for miles, and it was miserable.

Dreadful hills and a bad rocky stream to cross.
Samuel James, August 18, 1850

After inching down steep volcanic hills to the John Day River, the shallowness of the ford was welcome but its cobblestone-like bottom made the crossing difficult; there was no secure footing among the grey slippery rocks.

The Willamette Valley seemed elusively distant when the overlanders passed through this bleak unfriendly country, yet, from here, their destination was less than 100 miles away.

Me think if this be Oregon it is not the place I started for.
John Tully Kerns, September, 1852

After reaching the Dalles, the emigrants had to choose between finishing their journey by the treacherous, and expensive, water passage down the Columbia River, or a longer, no less hazardous land route using the Barlow Road, which crossed the Cascade Range on the southern flank of Mount Hood.

The craft used for the harrowing voyage down the Columbia were either rafts, jerry-built boats of some sort, or dugout canoes. Most were inadequate to begin with and unstable when overloaded with people and their belongings. If wagons were not sold at the Dalles they were lashed onto log rafts that were barely afloat with their heavy burdens. Livestock was herded along a precipitous trail, on the cliffs that paralleled the river, through a forest so dense in places it was dark as night.

The free-running Columbia plunged over waterfalls, through rapids, and coursed its way amid rock-strewn channels. As if this were not enough, winds of gale force frequently funneled down the deep narrow gorge. Boats driven by the wind were forced onto the opposite shore or, worse, splintered and wrecked on rocks, since there were few places where a landing could be made. Often progress had to be halted for days until the winds abated.

This is hard looking country, the roaring falls on one side, high rocky bluffs on the other, high peak of the Cascades in front...

Maria Belshaw, September 19, 1853

We landed at Fort Vancouver, forty miles below the Cascade Falls. The buildings occupied as stores, warehouses, shops, residences, etc., make quite a village. The ground back for half a mile is elevated several hundred feet above the river. It is set with grass, and makes a very pretty appearance.

Overton Johnson and William H. Winter, 1843

Upon reaching the Hudson's Bay Company's Fort Vancouver, the hard part of the journey was over and vestiges of civilization were a welcome sight to the travel-weary pioneers. Even the simplest of things, that had been everyday occurrences before they left home, caused comment. One young lady said succinctly: "Ate on a table. Slept in a house." Another, savoring the food he was offered, wrote: "She gave me an apple and a piece of bread and butter. Maybe you think it wasn't good."

Dr. John McLoughlin, the fort's chief factor, was always willing to do everything within his power to help the emigrants get settled. He not only gave them advice, but food, clothing, or other supplies they might need. Whether or not they could pay for what they received made no difference to this compassionate man. The Hudson's Bay Company disapproved of his beneficence toward the very people who were trying to displace England in the territory, so Dr. McLoughlin retired in 1846 and became an American citizen. For the next nine years, until his death in 1857, he continued to aid new settlers from his residence in Oregon City on the Willamette River.

Those who wanted nothing to do with frail rafts and flimsy boats on the Columbia River, and opted for the Barlow Road, had yet another long pull onto the high basalt plateau that rose sharply from the Dalles. Once on the heights they were rewarded with a view of Mount Hood rising in magnificent solitude to the southwest.

Within a few miles, deep narrow canyons began to branch from near the edge of the Trail. Their steep sides were covered with a dense growth of oak. These were the first groves of deciduous trees most of the travelers had seen in nearly 2,000 miles.

After one or two days' travel from the Dalles, the plateau suddenly opened onto the inviting nestled Tygh Valley. Before it could be reached, however, the infamous Tygh Valley Grade had to be negotiated, for the only access to the valley was over the rounded shoulders of the high hills encircling it.

Descended one of the highest and longest hills we have saw
yet in our travels...

John Tully Kerns, September 22, 1852

A Kentuckian, Samuel K. Barlow, was one who refused to pay the high fees demanded by the boat operators on the Columbia River. He felt sure there was a passage through the mountains. He found a way or, rather, made it. He and the other men in his party literally hacked their way through the trees with a few dull rusty tools that were incredibly inadequate for the job they had to do. The felled trees were piled up at the edge of the road, and joined the deadfalls and other rotting moss-covered vegetation of the forest floor.

At first the Barlow Road was only wide enough for an oxen-pulled wagon to pass, and barely that. It wound its boulder-strewn way through closely packed trees in the dank gloominess that pervades where no sunlight ever reaches the ground. On and on, upward the road tortuously went, with scarcely a break in the trees, to its summit of 4,000 feet on the angling slope of Mount Hood itself.

Drove twelve miles, crossing several small streams, and winding our way over roots, stumps, logs, brush, pole bridges, through mud holes, and across marshy swales in the forest.

John Tully Kerns, September 28, 1852

A break in the seemingly interminable forest at Summit Meadow was one of the few places where Mount Hood could be seen along the Barlow Road. Often the mountain wore a mantle of clouds and was obscured even from this closeness, at its very base; the tip of its cone was less than seven miles away. All admired the spectacle nature had created, but they had other feelings about the campground as they tried to make themselves comfortable for the night in the boggy, miry, cold dampness of the meadow.

Here we found good grass but the most terrible mud we had yet met with during the whole two thousand miles of travel.

P. V. Crawford, September 14, 1851

When we came to Laurel Hill we viewed that descent in alarm. It looked as if we had come to the jumping off place. It seemed almost perpendicular and such a long descent . . . The locked wheels made a most dismal screeching sound that echoed back and forth through the woods.

Adrietta Applegate Hixon, 1852

Earlier on, those who had seen what they thought was the worst hill in the world, changed their minds when they saw Laurel Hill falling away at their feet. It was almost as if Providence had arranged one final test of the emigrants' worthiness to settle in the promised land of Oregon.

On the Barlow Road, Laurel Hill, less than 50 miles from Oregon City and the end of the Oregon Trail, was, for several years, the only way down from the heights of the Cascades. The pioneers, long since bone-weary, weak, debilitated, and often hungry for their food supply was nearly gone, had yet to confront this awesome slope.

The descent was made in two sections; the worst was the first slope with a more vertical than horizontal grade of 60 percent. A level bench, which offered a few minutes where the travelers could catch their breath, led to the second hill which was not so steep.

It was impossible to take the wagons down the hill by traversing it because of their inability to make any sort of a sharp right-angle turn. They had to go over the brink and straight down the chute which was covered with scree—loose slippery unstable rocks.

Usually the teams were unyoked and taken down separately by way of a steep narrow winding trail. In some cases the wagons were slid down the incline after their wheels had been removed. Another method used was to lock the wheels, tie ropes to the wagon, snub the ropes around tree trunks, and pay them out, little by little, as the wagon was eased down. Trees 40 feet high, with many branches, were cut down and tied to the back of the wagons, where, it was hoped, their drag would serve to brake the wagons. The trees piled up at the bottom of the hill and made an effective stop for wagons that broke away. All the precautions were not enough for one man who said he went down Laurel Hill "like shot off a shovel."

As if the precipitous drop alone was not enough, an additional worry plagued the miserable travelers; the hungry oxen had to be continually watched to keep them from eating the leaves of the rhododendron—mistakenly called laurel—which was poisonous.

Samuel Barlow was given authorization to charge a toll for use of the road he had constructed, and he located the tollgate at the road's western terminus.

Having just traveled over the rough primitive road, the emigrants were in no mood to pay for the privilege of having done so. It was not long before Barlow moved the toll collection point to the beginning of the road, east of the Cascades.

Once through the western tollgate the pioneers were down off the mountain and only 40 miles from their destination at Oregon City. There was nothing ahead to daunt the now hardened travelers—only the rugged dizzying elevated Devil's Backbone section that would bring them to the crossing of, first, the Sandy River and then the Clackamas River. These would have been major obstacles, and would have caused some consternation, had they been encountered at the beginning of the Oregon Trail. Here, after all the many miles, they were mere nuisances.

Almost through with a long and tiresome journey of almost six months. Taking all things into consideration had a pleasant trip.

George N. Taylor, October 9, 1853

Relief and elation were coupled with near exhaustion after the emigrants finally had traversed the last mile of the Oregon Trail. They had made it. Not without problems, and not without some tragedy, but they had done it.

Now it was time to get on about the business of living.

I cannot realize that I am in a measure at my journey's
end, with peace and plenty all around.

Esther Belle Hanna, September 16, 1852

I now took off my blanket dress and put on my spick
and span new dress and corded bonnet which I had car-
ried safely on my saddle, and thus arrayed I staggered
to the door. Mrs. Hatch caught me in her arms and her
first words were, "Why dear woman, I supposed your
clothing had been torn off your body long ago."

Sarah J. Cummins, 1845

Went into a house to live again. The first one I had been
in since we crossed the Missouri. H. nearly wild with
joy. Did not want to camp out again.

Lucia Loraine Williams, September 3, 1851

Friday, October 27. Arrived at Oregon City at the falls
of the Willamette.

Saturday, October 28. Went to work.

James W. Nesmith, 1843

PHOTOGRAPH LOCATIONS

Below are the locations for each Oregon Trail photograph. A map is on the following pages. Each site on the map is identified by the page number on which the photograph appears.

Only general locations are shown. For more precise locating, individual state maps should be consulted.

Each photograph that contains visible Oregon Trail ruts is noted.

79 Church Buttes, Wyoming: *12 miles southwest of Granger, Wyoming.*

80 Fort Bridger State Historic Site, Wyoming: *in town of Fort Bridger, Wyoming.*

82 Muddy Creek, Wyoming: *14 miles south of Kemmerer, Wyoming; 1 mile east of Highway 189.*

IDAHO

84 Thomas Fork, Bear River Valley, Idaho: *1 mile west of Border, Wyoming, on Highway 30.*

85 Bear River Valley, Idaho: *6 miles south of Montpelier, Idaho, on Highway 30.*

86, 87 Soda Springs, Idaho: *in town of Soda Springs, Idaho.*

88, 89 Alexander Crater, Idaho: *8 miles west of Soda Springs, Idaho, on Highway 30.*

91 Fort Hall, Idaho: *Ross Park, Pocatello, Idaho.*

92 Massacre Rocks State Park, Idaho: *10 miles west of American Falls, Idaho, on Interstate 86.*

93 Cauldron Linn, Snake River, Idaho: *2 miles east of Murtaugh, Idaho. Viewpoint on private property.*

94 Shoshone Falls, Idaho: *3 miles east of Twin Falls, Idaho.*

95 Rock Creek, Idaho: *½ mile southeast of city limits of Twin Falls, Idaho.*

96 Thousand Springs, Idaho: *6 miles south of Hagerman, Idaho, on Highway 30.*

97 Above Three Island Crossing, Idaho: *Across Snake River opposite Three Island Crossing State Park, near Glenn's Ferry, Idaho. Ruts.*

99 Three Island Crossing State Park, Idaho: *2 miles southwest of Glenn's Ferry, Idaho.*

100, 101 Bruneau Dunes State Park, Idaho: *14 miles west of Hammett, Idaho.*

102 Bonneville Point, Idaho: *8¾ miles southeast of Boise, Idaho; 3½ miles north of Interstate 84. Ruts.*

103 Canyon Hill, Idaho: *1 mile north of Caldwell, Idaho.*

104 Snake River, Fort Boise, Idaho: *2 miles north of Parma, Idaho.*

OREGON and WASHINGTON

105 Lytle Pass, Oregon: *5 miles south of Vale, Oregon. Ruts.*

106 Farewell Bend State Park, Oregon: *5 miles south of Huntington, Oregon.*

107 Burnt River, Oregon: *Weatherby Rest Area on Interstate 84, 3 miles north of Lime, Oregon.*

108 Ladd Canyon Hill, Grande Ronde Valley, Oregon: *Ladd Canyon Rest Area on Interstate 84, 5 miles south of La Grande, Oregon.*

109 Blue Mountains, Oregon: *9 miles northwest of La Grande, Oregon.*

110 Grande Ronde River Crossing, Oregon: *Hilgard Junction State Park on Interstate 84, 9 miles northwest of La Grande, Oregon.*

111 Mount Adams from Deadman Pass, Oregon: *19 miles southeast of Pendleton, Oregon, on Interstate 84.*

112 Emigrant Hill, Oregon: *6 miles east of Mission, Oregon. Ruts.*

113 Whitman Mission National Historic Site, Washington: *7 miles west of Walla Walla, Washington, on Highway 12.*

114 Upper Well Spring, Oregon: *15 miles west of Butler Junction, Oregon.*

115 John Day River Crossing, Oregon: *12 miles southwest of Shutler, Oregon.*

116 Columbia Plateau, Oregon: *south of Biggs, Oregon, on Highway 97.*

118 Columbia River, Oregon: *near North Bonneville, Washington.*

119 Multnomah Falls, Oregon: *14 miles west of Cascade Locks, Oregon, on Highway 30.*

120, 121 Fort Vancouver National Historic Site, Washington: *Vancouver, Washington.*

122 Tygh Valley, Oregon: *town of Tygh Valley, Oregon. Ruts.*

124 Barlow Road near Barlow Pass, Oregon: *U.S. Forest Service Road 3530, 12 miles west of Wamic, Oregon. Ruts.*

125 Barlow Road below Laurel Hill, Oregon: *Trail off Highway 26. Ruts.*

127, 128 Summit Meadow, Oregon: *Still Creek Campground Road, off Highway 26 near Government Camp, Oregon.*

129, 131 Laurel Hill, Oregon: *2 miles west of Government Camp, Oregon, on Highway 26. Ruts.*

132 Barlow Road Tollgate, Oregon: *Rhododendron, Oregon, on Highway 26. Ruts.*

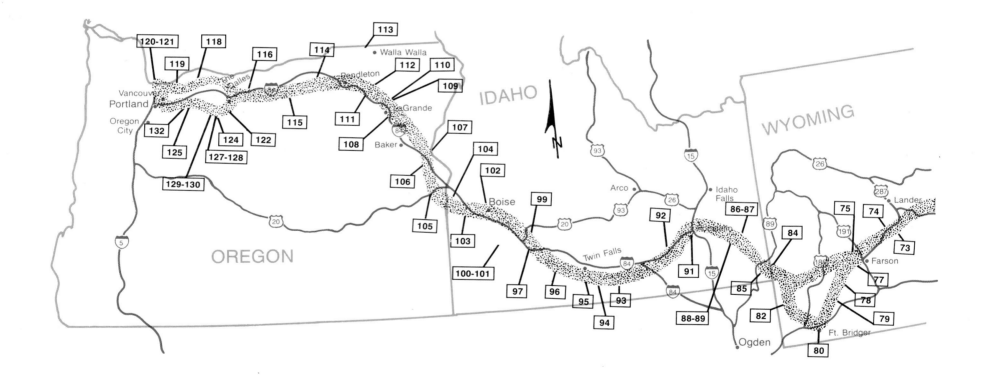

120-121 118 113

119 116 114

Walla Walla

112 110

IDAHO

109

Vancouver Pendleton

Portland LaGrande

Oregon 132 111 WYOMING

City 124 122 107

125 115 104

127-128 108 Baker 102 75 74

Lander

129-130 106 105 99 Arco 86-87 84

Boise 92 Idaho 73

103 20 Falls 89 191

100-101 Twin Falls 91 85 Farson

97 96 93 84 88-89 82 77

95 94 Ogden Ft. Bridger 78

80 79

OREGON

N

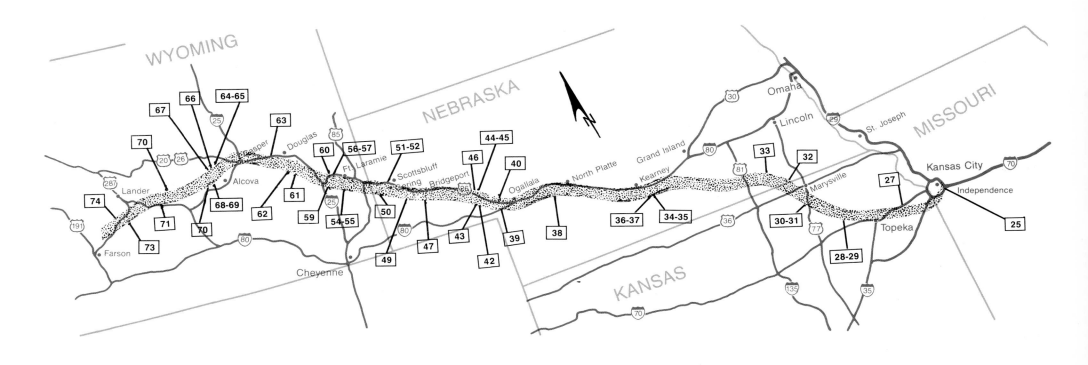

WYOMING

NEBRASKA

MISSOURI

KANSAS

66

64-65

67

63

70

60 56-57 51-52 44-45

46

40

33 32

27

74

61 50

38

36-37 34-35

30-31

25

68-69

62 59 54-55

71 70

73

49 47 43 39

42

28-29

Casper

Douglas

Alcova

Ft. Laramie

Scottsbluff

Bridgeport

Ogallala

North Platte

Grand Island

Kearney

Marysville

Topeka

Independence

Kansas City

Omaha

Lincoln

St. Joseph

Lander

Farson

Cheyenne

139

BIBLIOGRAPHY

Adams, Cecilia Emily McMillen, Diary, Oregon Historical Society Manuscript Library,* Mss. 1508.

Atkin, James, Journal, O.H.S.M.L., Mss. 1508

Allyn, Henry A., *A Record of Daily Events During a Trip From Fulton County, Illinois, Across the Plains to the Willamette Valley, Oregon Territory in the Year 1853,* O.H.S.M.L., Mss. 1508.

Alt, David D. and Hyndman, Donald W., *Roadside Geology of Oregon,* Missoula, Montana, Mountain Press Publishing Company, 1981.

Anderson, William Wright, Diary, O.H.S.M.L., Mss. 1508.

Applegate, Jesse, *A Day With the Cow Column in 1843,* Oregon Historical Quarterly,** Vol. 1, December 1900.

Applegate, Virginia Watson, *Barlow Road,* 1849, O.H.S.M.L., Mss. 233.

Bailey, Walter, *The Barlow Road,* O.H.Q., Vol. 13, September 1912.

Barlow, William, *Reminiscences of Seventy Years,* O.H.Q., Vol. 13, September 1912.

Beal, Josiah, Narrative, 1847, O.H.S.M.L., Mss. 1508.

Beckham, Dr. Stephen Dow, *The Barlow Road,* Gerald, Missouri, The Overland Journal, Vol. 2, No. 3, Summer 1984.

Belshaw, Maria Parsons, Diary, 1853, O.H.Q., Vol. 33, December 1932.

Boardman, John, *The Overland Journey from Kansas to Oregon in 1843,* Utah Historical Quarterly, Vol. 2, October 1929.

Boone, George L., Sketch of 1848 trip, O.H.S.M.L., Mss. 1508.

Bowman, Frank, Diary, 1844-1872, O.H.S.M.L., Mss. 1491.

Brown, John, Journal, O.H.S.M.L., Mss. 2363.

Bruff, J. Goldsborough, Diary, 1849, Yale Collection of Western Americana, Ms.50.

Buckingham, Harriet T., O.H.S.M.L., Mss. 1156.

Burnett, Peter H., Letters, 1844, O.H.Q., Vol. 3, March 1902.

Butler, Mrs., *1853 Diary of the Rogue River Valley,* Oscar Osburn Winther and Rose Dodge, O.H.Q., Vol. 41, December 1940.

Carey, Charles H. (ed.), *The Journals of Theodore Talbot,* Portland, Oregon, Metropolitan Press, 1931.

Carnahan, Mary Ellen Morrison, Recollections, O.H.S.M.L., Mss. 1177.

Castle, Gwen, *Belshaw Journey, Oregon Trail, 1853,* O.H.Q., Vol. 32, September 1931.

Chambers, Margaret White, Reminiscences, O.H.S.M.L., Mss. 1508.

Churchill, Claire Warner, (intro. and ed.), *The Journey to Oregon—A Pioneer Girl's Diary,* O.H.Q., Vol. 29, March 1928.

Clackamas County Historical Society and Wasco County Historical Society, *Barlow Road,* Portland, Oregon, 1976.

Clark, Thomas D., *Frontier America, The Story of the Westward Movement,* New York, New York, Charles Scribner's Sons, 1959.

Condit, Philip, Diary, 1854, O.H.S.M.L., Mss. 922.

Condit, Sylvanus, Diary, 1854, O.H.S.M.L., Mss. 923.

Cooper, A. A., *Our Journey Across the Plains from Missouri to Oregon, 1863,* O.H.S.M.L., Mss. 1508.

Cornell, William, Diary, O.H.S.M.L., Mss. 290.

Cranston, Sarah Marsh, Daily Journal, O.H.S.M.L., Mss. 674.

Crawford, P. V., *Journal of a Trip Across the Plains, 1851,* O.H.Q., Vol. 25, June 1924.

Cross, Osborne, ed. by Raymond W. Settle, *The March of the Mounted Riflemen,* Glendale, California, Arthur H. Clark, 1940.

Cummins, Sarah J., O.H.S.M.L., Mss. 1508.

Davidson, Albert Franklin, Speech and *Journal of Exploration in the Willamette Valley in Fall and Winter, 1845-46,* O.H.S.M.L., Mss. 386.

Deady, Lucy Ann (Mrs. Matthew P.), *Crossing the Plains to Oregon in 1846,* O.H.S.M.L., Mss. 48.

Dement, Russell C., and Ellis S., ed. by E. R. Jackman, *After the Covered Wagons,* O.H.Q., Vol. 63, March 1962.

DeVoto, Bernard, *Across the Wide Missouri,* Boston, Massachusetts, Houghton Mifflin Company, 1947.

Dowell, Benjamin Franklin, *Journal, Missouri to California 1850,* O.H.S.M.L., Mss. 209

Dudley, Mrs. Sarah Francis Mrs., *Trip Across the Plains, 1852,* O.H.S.M.L., Mss. 1508.

Duniway, Abigail Jane, Overland Diary, 1852, O.H.S.M.L., Mss. 432.

Earl, Robert, Reminiscences, 1845, O.H.S.M.L., Mss. 793.

Eaton, Herbert, *The Overland Trail to California in 1852,* New York, New York, G.P. Putnam's Sons, 1974.

Faris, John T., *On the Trail of the Pioneers,* New York, New York, George H. Doran Company, 1920.

Field, James, *Crossing the Plains,* O.H.S.M.L., Mss. 520.

Findley, William C., Diary, O.H.S.M.L., Mss. 494.

Fisher, Rev. Ezra, Correspondence, ed. by Sarah Fisher Henderson, Nellie E. Latourette, and Kenneth S. Latourette, O.H.Q., Vol. 16, December 1915.

Franzwa, Gregory M., *The Oregon Trail Revisited,* Gerald, Missouri, Patrice Press, Inc., 1983.

Franzwa, Gregory M., *Maps of the Oregon Trail,* Gerald, Missouri, Patrice Press, Inc., 1982.

Fremont, John Charles, ed. by Donald Jackson and Mary Lee Spence, *Expeditions of John Charles Fremont, 1843,* Urbana, Illinois, University of Illinois Press, 1970.

Fry, John O., *A Trip Across the Plains,* O.H.S.M.L., Mss. 427.

Gaylord, Orange, Overland Journey, 1853, O.H.S.M.L., Mss. 726.

Ghent, W. J., *The Road to Oregon, A Chronicle of the Great Emigrant Trail,* London, New York, and Toronto, Longmans, Green and Co., 1929.

Gibson, James, *Missouri to Oregon, 1847,* O.H.S.M.L., Mss. 141.

Glenn, John G., Diary, O.H.S.M,L, Mss. 284.

Goltra, Mrs. E. J., Journal, 1853, O.H.S.M.L., Mss. 1508.

Hadley, Amelia, O.H.S.M.L., Mss. 253.

Haines, Aubrey L., *Historic Sites Along the Oregon Trail,* Gerald, Missouri, Patrice Press, Inc., 1981.

Hancock, Samuel, intro. by Arthur D. Howden-Smith, Narrative, 1845, New York, New York, R. M. McBride and Co., 1927.

Handsaker, Samuel, *Oregon Trail, 1853,* Eugene, Oregon, Lane County Pioneer Historical Society, 1965 (orig. pub. in Alton Telegraph, Alton, Illinois).

Hanna, Esther Belle, Diary, 1852, O.H.S.M.L., Mss. 1508.

Hanna, William, *Diary, Illinois to California, 1850,* O.H.S.M.L., Mss. 693.

Harden, Absolom B., *Trail Diary, 1847,* O.H.S.M.L., Mss. 11.

Harrison, J. M., Account of Journey, 1846, O.H.S.M.L., Mss. 1508.

Harritt, Jesse H., O.H.S.M.L., Mss. 947.

Hastings, Loren B., Journal, O.H.S.M.L., Mss. 660.

Hayden, Mary Jane, *Pioneer Days,* O.H.S.M.L., Mss. 1508.

Hemey, John Bunker, Diary, 1864, O.H.S.M.L., Mss. 2605.

Herren, John, *A Diary of 1845,* O.H.S.M.L., Mss. 224.

Hewitt, Randall H., *Across the Plains and Over the Divide,* New York, New York, Argosy Antiquarian Ltd., 1964.

Hill, Mrs. Sarah Almoran, *Journey to Oregon in 1843,* O.H.S.M.L., Mss. 1508.

Hite, Joseph, Diary, O.H.S.M.L., Mss. 1508.

Hixon, Adrietta Applegate, *On to Oregon,* O.H.S.M.L., Mss. 1508.

Hockett, William A., O.H.S.M.L., Mss. 1036.

Holmes, Kenneth L., *Covered Wagon Women,* Vols. I, II, III, Glendale, California, Arthur H. Clark Co., 1983.

Hooker, William Francis, *The Prairie Schooner,* Chicago, Illinois, Saul Brothers, 1918.

Howell, John Ewing, Journal, 1845, O.H.S.M.L., Mss. 659.

Hunt, G. W., *To Oregon by Ox Team, 1847,* O.H.S.M.L., Mss. 1508.

Hunt, Nancy A., *By Ox-Team to California,* O.H.S.M.L., Mss. 1508.

Idaho Historical Society, Bicentennial Commission, *Route of the Oregon Trail in Idaho,* Boise, Idaho, 1974.

James, Samuel, *Trip from Iowa to Oregon,* O.H.S.M.L., Mss. 1508.

Johnson, Overton, and Winter, William H., O.H.Q., Vol. 7, March 1906.

Kahler, William, Journal, 1852, Yale Collection of Western Americana, Ms.277.

Kerns, John Tully, Diary, 1852, O.H.S.M.L., Mss. 1508.

Ketcham, Rebecca, *From Ithaca to Clatsop Plains: Miss Ketcham's Journal of Travels,* O.H.Q., Vol. 42, September 1961 and December 1961.

Lee, Anna Green, O.H.S.M.L., Mss. 283.

Lockley, Fred, *Reminiscences of James E. R. Harrell,* O.H.Q., Vol. 24, June 1923.

Lockley, Fred, *Recollections of Benjamin Franklin Bonney,* O.H.Q., Vol. 24, March 1923.

Long, Mary Jane, *Crossing the Plains in the Year of 1852 with Ox Teams,* O.H.S.M.L., Mss. 1508.

Longmire, James, O.H.S.M.L., Mss. 1004.

Longworth, Basil N., *Diary, 1853,* Denver, Colorado, D.E. Harrington, 1927.

Martin, Charles W., *The Alcove Spring,* Gerald, Missouri, Overland Journal, Vol. 2, No. 1, Winter 1984.

Mattes, Merrill J., *The Great Platte River Road,* Lincoln, Nebraska, Nebraska State Historical Society, 1969.

McCall, A. J., *The Great California Trail in 1849,* (reprint from Steuben Courier, Steuben, New York, 1882) O.H.S.M.L., Mss. 1508.

McClung, James S., Diary, 1862, O.H.S.M.L., Mss. 1508

McClure, Andrew S., O.H.S.M.L., Mss. 732B.

McDannald, David Walker, Diary, O.H.S.M.L., Mss. 1508

McKaig, Silas, Diary, 1852, O.H.S.M.L., Mss. 151.

McKean, Samuel Terry, Reminiscences, 1847, O.H.S.M.L., Mss. 483.

McNary, Lawrence A., *Route of the Meek Cut-off, 1845,* and quotes from Jessie Harritt Diary, O.H.Q., Vol. 35, March 1934.

Meeker, Ezra, *The Ox Team, or the Old Oregon Trail,* Omaha, Nebraska, Ezra Meeker, 1907.

Miller, James D., *Early Oregon Scenes: A Pioneer Narrative,* O.H.Q., Vol. 31, March 1930.

Minto, Hon. John, *Reminiscences of a Pioneer of 1844,* O.H.Q., Vol. 2, June 1901.

Moreland, Rev., Jesse, *Journey of 1852,* O.H.S.M.L., Mss. 1508.

Morfitt, William, *Memories of '47,* O.H.S.M.L., Mss. 1508.

Munger, Asahel, and wife, Diary, 1839, O.H.Q., Vol. 8, December 1907.

Musil, Faye, *Overland Forts,* Lincoln, Nebraska, Nebraskaland, Vol. 59, No. 13, September 1981.

Myres, Sandra L., *Ho For California,* San Marino, California, Henry E. Huntington Library and Art Gallery, 1980.

National Geographic Society, *Trails West,* Washington, D.C., 1979.

Nebraska Game and Parks Commission, *The Oregon Trail.*

Nesmith, James W., *Diary of the Emigration of 1843,* O.H.Q., Vol. 7, December 1906.

Newby, William T., O.H.Q., Vol. 40, September 1939.

Oakly, Obadiah, *Expedition to Oregon, 1842,* O.H.S.M.L., Mss. 1508.

Pabian, Roger K., and Swinehart, II, James B., *Geologic History of Scott's Bluff National Monument,* Lincoln, Nebraska, Conservation and Survey Division, Institute of Agriculture and Natural Resources, University of Nebraska, 1979.

Paden, Irene D., *The Wake of the Prairie Schooner,* Carbondale and Edwardsville, Illinois, Southern Illinois University Press, 1970.

Palmer, Harriet Scott, *Crossing Over the Great Plains by Ox Wagons, 1852,* O.H.S.M.L., Mss. 1508.

Palmer, Joel *Journal of Travels Over the Rocky Mountains 1845-1846,* in Early Western Travels, Thwaites, Cleveland, Ohio, Arthur H. Clark, Vol. 30, 1906.

Parker, Rev. Samuel, *Journal of an Exploring Tour Beyond the Rocky Mountains,* Ithaca, New York, Mack, Andrus, and Woodruff, 1842.

Parker, Samuel, Diary, 1845, O.H.S.M.L., Mss. 1508.

Parkman, Francis, *The Oregon Trail,* Garden City, New York, Doubleday and Co., 1946.

Patterson, Laura A. Hawn, Recollections, 1843, O.H.S.M.L., Mss. 381.

Pattison, William, Diary, O.H.S.M.L., Mss. 1072.

Pease, David Egbert, Diary, 1849, O.H.S.M.L., Mss. 60.

Pengra, Charlotte Stearns, Diary, 1853, Eugene, Oregon, Lane County Pioneer Historical Society.

Pfouts, Paris Swazey, O.H.S.M.L., Mss. 297.

Pringle, Catharine Sager, Recollections, O.H.S.M.L., Mss. 1194-1.

Pringle, Virgil, Diary, O.H.S.M.L., Mss. 1194.

Raynor, James, O.H.S.M.L., Mss. 1508.

Reed, Henry E., *Lovejoy's Pioneer Narrative,* O.H.Q., Vol. 31, September 1930.

Reid, John Phillip, *Replenishing the Elephant,* from John Smith's travels, 1853, O.H.Q., Vol. 79, Spring 1978.

Renshaw, Robert Harvey, Diary, O.H.S.M.L., Mss. 418.

Robe, Rev. Robert, Diary, 1851, O.H.S.M.L., Mss. 1163.

Rogers, Martha Ellen, Reminiscences, O.H.S.M.L., Mss. 697.

Ruddell, W. H., *Trip Across the Plains, 1851,* O.H.S.M.L., Mss. 1508.

Sage, Rufus B., Letters, papers and *Scenes in the Rocky Mountains,* two volumes, Glendale, California, Arthur H. Clark, 1956.

Sargent, Elisha Nelson, O.H.S.M.L., Mss. 813.

Saunders, Delila Berintha, Diary, 1866, O.H.S.M.L., Mss. 1508.

Scott, Charlton, Diary, 1862, O.H.S.M.L., Mss. 1054B.

Smith, Elizabeth Dixon, O.H.S.M.L., Mss. 641.

Spaulding, Kenneth A. (ed.), *On the Old Oregon Trail, Robert Stuart's Journey of Discovery,* Norman Oklahoma, University of Oklahoma Press, 1953.

Spencer, John B., Diary, 1852, O.H.S.M.L., Mss. 1508.

Starbuck, Edith, *Crossing the Plains,* Nashville, Tennessee, Southern Publishing Association, 1927.

Starr, J. R., Diary from Iowa to Idaho, 1850, O.H.S.M.L., Mss. 2473.

Stevens, Charles, Letters, 1852, O.H.Q., Vol. 37, June 1936.

Stewart, George R., *The California Trail*, Lincoln, Nebraska, University of Nebraska Press, 1962.

Strachan, John, *Blazing the Millan Trail*, O.H.S.M.L., Mss. 1508.

Sutton, Sarah, Diary, O.H.S.M.L., Mss. 2280.

Taylor, George N., Diary, O.H.S.M.L., Mss. 1508.

Taylor, John S., Diary, 1854, O.H.S.M.L., Mss. 17.

Taylor, S. H., *Oregon Bound*, Letters to the Watertown Chronicle, Watertown, Wisconsin, O.H.Q., Vol. 22, June 1921.

Thomson, Origen, O.H.S.M.L., Mss. 1508.

Townsend, John Kirk, *The Overland Journeys of John H. Wyeth and John Kirk Townsend*, Fairfield, Washington, Ye Galleon Press, 1970.

Unruh, John D., Jr., *The Plains Across*, Urbana, Illinois, University of Illinois Press, 1982.

Vanbuskirk, William, Diary, 1852, O.H.S.M.L., Mss. 881.

Ward, D.B., *Across the Plains in 1853*, O.H.S.M.L., Mss. 1508.

Ware, Joseph, E., *The Emigrant's Guide to California*, Princeton, New Jersey, Princeton University Press, 1932.

Warren, Daniel Knight, Reminiscences, O.H.Q., Vol. 3, September 1902.

West, Calvin B., Journal and letters, 1853, O.H.S.M.L., Mss. 692.

West, George Miller, *Crossing the Plains*, O.H.S.M.L., Mss. 1508.

Wigle, Abraham J., Account of overland journey, 1852, O.H.S.M.L., Mss. 587.

Williams, Veleria A., Journal, O.H.S.M.L., Mss. 1508.

Wood, Elizabeth, *Journal of a Trip to Oregon, 1851*, O.H.Q., Vol. 27, March 1926.

Wood, Tallmadge B., Letter, O.H.Q., Vol. 3, March 1902.

Woodcock, William C., Diary, O.H.S.M.L., Mss. 982.

Wyeth, John B. *The Overland Journey of John B. Wyeth and John Kirk Townsend*, Fairfield, Washington, Ye Galleon Press, 1970.

Young, John Quincy Adams, O.H.S.M.L., Mss. 187.

Zieber, John S., *Journal, Peoria, Illinois to Oregon City, 1851*, O.H.S.M.L., Mss. 1508.

ABOUT THE AUTHORS

Bill and Jan Moeller are photographers, writers, and avid travelers who combine their journeys and mutual skills with their interest in history.

The Moellers both were born in Omaha, Nebraska. When they were young adults they moved to New York City. There Bill worked as a photographer and filmmaker. Many of his motion pictures won national and international awards. Jan was an art director, freelance writer, and photographer.

After many years they decided to become full-time travelers since their demanding careers allowed them little time for exploring the historic places they wanted to see.

They have since journeyed over many historic trails, paths, and waterways. They have visited all the battlefields of the American Revolution and followed the Arnold Trail to Quebec, Canada. In their own sailboat they have cruised the length of the Intracoastal Waterway several times, and circumnavigated the eastern half of the United States, a voyage which took them across the Erie Canal from Albany to Buffalo, New York, through the Great Lakes, and down the Mississippi River, following in the wake of Mark Twain. Their latest journey has been along the wagon ruts and swales of the Oregon Trail from Independence, Missouri, to Oregon City and the Willamette Valley in Oregon.

When reading about history the Moellers often felt the visual material was inadequate, especially regarding a subject where the land or terrain figured prominently or decisively. The history books that use merely engravings, romanticized paintings, or badly reproduced black and white photographs were not satisfying to them. They felt a new approach was needed, something that would fill a gap in the existing material on a given subject and provide it with another dimension. Hence this book, a visual journey along the Oregon Trail.

The Moellers have written three other books and numerous magazine articles, but this is the first book that features their splendid color photography.

As to where they reside now, it is wherever their travel-trailer-home is parked. It never stays in one place for very long, however, because they are continually traveling, gathering material for their future projects.